D0461208

ALAN THE CHRISTMAS DONKEY

Tracy Garton
with Danielle Hoffman

Alan the Christmas Donkey

The Little Donkey Who Made a Big Difference

SIDGWICK & JACKSON

First published 2016 by Sidgwick & Jackson
an imprint of Pan Macmillan
20 New Wharf Road, London N1 9RR
Associated companies throughout the world
www.panmacmillan.com

ISBN 978-1-5098-3902-5

1 3 5 7 9 8 6 4 2

A CIP catalogue record for this book is available from the British Library.

Typeset by Palimpsest Book Production Limited, Falkirk, Stirlingshire
Printed and bound by CPI Group (UK) Ltd, Croydon CR0 4YY

Visit **www.panmacmillan.com** to read more about all our books
and to buy them. You will also find features, author interviews and
news of any author events, and you can sign up for e-newsletters
so that you're always first to hear about our new releases.

*This book is dedicated to all the donkeys we have
rescued, for the joy and occasional heartbreak
they have brought us. There may be sleepless nights
spent in the stables with sick donkeys, but there is
great joy when they get better. There's also the joy of
chasing escaped donkeys around the village at 3 a.m.!
Bless them, they test us every day. We know we have
made a big difference to their lives and they have
certainly made a big difference to ours.*

Contents

Contents

Prologue

Most of us are lucky enough to have a special someone who, when we look back, we can say really has changed our life for the better. This could be a family member, a partner, an old friend, or even just a stranger we had a chance encounter with. I'm fortunate enough to have several special someones. I love my husband of thirty-three years dearly, but two of my most life-changing encounters have been with animals.

Twenty-five years ago now I came across a lonely, scraggy mule snuffling around in the dirt in a field just down the road from the house I then lived in by the River Trent in Nottinghamshire. I'd always been an animal lover and, as I looked into the creature's deep brown eyes, I felt a special connection. Somewhere, deep in my gut, I knew that I was there to change that mule's life.

Our special moment didn't last long – just minutes

later I was legging it back to the gate in fear for my life, with that scruffy animal in hot pursuit. Hardly an emotional Hollywood-style plot-changing scene. Yet, panting as I vaulted over the fence just in the nick of time, I realised I couldn't walk away and do nothing. I've always believed everyone deserves a friend. That goes for animals too. That mule needed a pal – and why shouldn't that be me?

Fast forward two decades, and I look back on my first encounter with Muffin, as he became named, with a smile. If only I'd known just how pivotal that moment would be. He was the founding resident at what would become the Radcliffe Donkey Sanctuary – and he wasn't the only resident for long. Since that day, I've somehow become a fierce protector of hundreds of mules, horses, donkeys, and even the odd zebra/donkey crossbreed thrown in for good measure. Up at 5.30 a.m. every day to start ticking off items on the never-ending jobs list at my sanctuary, it became easy to get bogged down in the financial struggles, health worries, and stresses that I've learned the hard way come with the territory.

But then, amid the rural rollercoaster of ups and downs, I met Alan. I'd like to say that I love each donkey equally – they certainly get equal care and attention. However, being completely honest, that wouldn't quite be true. I hold my hands up, I do have my favourites.

And when Alan came to live at the sanctuary it was only a matter of days before I realised he was special.

Alan was actually rescued shortly after Christmas, and I like to think that we gave him a festive miracle. He was in a desperate state and surely wishing for a better life, not one starved of the basics of nourishment, warmth and love. Then I came along, as his guardian angel. I shudder to think what would have happened if I hadn't turned up in time.

Not a day goes by when my lovely Alan doesn't make me smile but as you're about to see, he's also given me more than his fair share of trouble with his cheeky antics – escape plots, public displays of embarrassment and a tug of war with a model's bikini bottoms to name just a few of his escapades . . . But he also saved the life of his friend and gave me the greatest Christmas gift of all.

However, before I tell you more about Alan, let me take you back to the beginning.

1

Lost and Found

As I stretched out in bed, the piercing bell of my alarm clock shattered the silence. My eyes were still bleary from sleep but, squinting, I could just about make out the time. It was 6 a.m., time to give the animals their breakfast. And, as if by clockwork, I could hear four-legged footsteps bounding up the stairs towards me.

'I'm coming, I'm coming,' I called, scurrying from the warmth of the duvet into my snuggly purple dressing gown.

I opened the door a crack and was greeted by a sloppy tongue licking my hand, with another cold nose snuffling around my bare feet.

'Get down, Jenna, and that's enough, Rumpole,' I said, pushing my German pointer's soft brown head away, and stepping out of the reach of my tubby white bulldog.

It was hardly a relaxing wake-up call, but this was a pretty typical morning. With three dogs – Jenna, Rumpole and my darling Italian spinone, Ben – two attention-seeking cats – Sooty and Maxwell – and two tortoises – Walter and Betty – out on the lawn as well, my porridge would have to wait.

I'd always been an animal lover, and when my husband, Steve, and I got married in 1983 we decided not to have children. Just as some couples always know they'll start a family, we felt sure it wasn't for us. Instead, we filled our lovely three-bed detached home with furry friends. Steve only had a budgie before he met me, bless him. I'd always known I wanted a house full of pets, though.

As a child, I'd drive my parents mad by sneaking any creature I could get my hands on back into my bedroom. Injured birds, lost mice, even a bat, I wasn't fussy. Living in the Nottinghamshire countryside, there was always an animal that I could convince myself desperately needed my help. So I'd scoop them up in my school jumper, and snuggle them safely on top of the pile of books in my school bag.

Getting past my mum was always the first hurdle, and eventually I adopted the strategy of dashing straight upstairs muttering something about homework. Looking back, that probably set her alarm bells ringing immediately, if my old school reports are anything to go by. I wasn't exactly the studious type. I spent more time gazing longingly out of the window than paying attention to the blackboard.

However, once upstairs with my bedroom door closed behind me, I had the next part of the plan down to a fine art. I kept a cardboard box in the bottom of my wardrobe at the ready for my next animal rescue. So, as silent as the mice I would bring home, I'd creak open the doors and deposit my latest find into its new home.

Inevitably, my mum would find out and, with the exception of one lucky mouse, my little friends would always be turfed back outside. For some reason I got away with keeping Mickey, and he spent the next few years living happily in a cage on my desk.

By the time I reached my teens, my nurturing instincts hadn't gone away. In fact, I decided that I wanted to be a vet. I loved the idea of spending all day with animals, and was already daydreaming about swooping in wearing my white veterinary coat and saving the day. However, I'd given much less thought to the qualifications I'd need. My heart sank when our school careers adviser listed the exams I'd have to take, and the years at university I'd need to commit to.

Soon I discovered boys and make-up, and my dreams of being a vet faded away. Instead I thought maybe I'd be a hairdresser. It sounded glam, and I thought I could always care for animals in my spare time. In the meantime, I took a part-time after-school job in a fish and chip shop, and that's how, in 1980, I met Steve.

How I managed to appear alluring amid the grease and the strong fishy smell, I'll never know. I recognised Steve from school, but as he was a few years older we didn't really know each other. However, after that first night when our eyes met over the chippy counter, we'd always say hello when we bumped into each other out and about. Getting the attention of an older lad was a bit of a coup, and I felt pretty chuffed with myself. I liked his cheeky sense of humour, and I thought he was the best-looking guy in town. Blond hair and a twinkle in his eye, just my type. Then, to my surprise, a passing nod turned into a brief chat and, eventually, one evening Steve plucked up the courage to ask me out.

Three years later we'd tied the knot, and by 1988 we'd moved from Woodthorpe near Nottingham into our dream three-bed detached home in Bailey Lane at the quiet edge of Radcliffe-on-Trent. The peaceful country-side setting was idyllic, and we loved village life. There was a small parade of shops, a decent selection of beers on tap at our local pub, the Black Lion, and fresh air in abundance.

By now, my hairdressing ambitions were long gone. I'd done the training and, after just a few weeks' working in a local salon, I'd realised it wasn't all it was cracked up to be. I wasn't living the dream creating glamorous up-dos or experimenting with the latest colour trends. In reality, I was washing and perming old ladies' hair while faking an intense interest in how the weather had been lately and the week they'd booked in Spain.

After that I spent seven or eight years in the jewellery business, working in shops in Nottingham, Grantham and Leicester. The money was good, and I actually enjoyed learning all about the different gemstones and how to decode a hallmark. Soon enough, though, I began to get bored. Instead, I started working for my mum and stepdad, who owned a small chain of video rental stores in Radcliffe-on-Trent and West Bridgford.

On one particular day, a Friday in 1991, I'd spent a long afternoon in the shop helping customers to choose their movies for the weekend. The best part of my job was watching previews of the films so we could select which we wanted to stock, so I was always ready with a recommendation or two. Back then it cost around £100 for us to buy in each new release, so it was a big responsibility making sure we only shelled out for the good ones. Eventually, the last rental had been booked out and I headed straight over to the Chinese takeaway in the Radcliffe-on-Trent high street to pick up a late dinner for me and Steve. It was our regular weekend treat, unless we fancied heading into Nottingham to our favourite curry house.

'I hope you've got some prawn crackers in there,' Steve said, as I nudged open the kitchen door and set the bag of greasy goodies down on the table.

'Of course! I'm absolutely starving,' I replied.

Steve was still tugging off his work boots, having worked late in his job as a travelling printer-engineer. Soon, though, we were perched on the sofa with full, steaming plates on our laps and some nonsense on the telly in the background.

'Before I forget, I spotted something interesting on the way home,' Steve said, between mouthfuls of chicken chop suey.

'Oh yeah, what's that then?'

'Well, you know that field just before you arrive in the next village? I reckon it's got a donkey or something in it,' he said. 'It was too dark to get a proper look, but I think he was on his own. I hope he's all right. I felt a bit sorry for him really.'

It was early March, and the weather had been particularly cold and wet. Like Steve, I didn't like to think of a donkey out there in the frost either.

'I'll pop over tomorrow on the way to work, just to check on him,' I said, chewing thoughtfully on a forkful of sweet and sour king prawns.

We settled down to a night of channel flicking through the telly. Neither of us are big TV fans, and after a long afternoon in the video shop I couldn't stomach a movie. However, that evening I don't think it would have mattered what we were watching. I just couldn't concentrate. My mind kept drifting back to the conversation with Steve, and I was imagining that poor, sad donkey in a field all on his own. There wasn't much I could do at that time of night, but if it hadn't been for the wintry darkness I would have driven down to the field there and then.

'I know what you're thinking, but he'll be fine until tomorrow,' Steve said, reading my thoughts. 'It's Friday night, relax.'

'I know, I know,' I said doubtfully.

I flicked the kettle on to make us each a cup of tea, telling myself that Steve was right. However, setting my alarm extra early for the morning wouldn't hurt.

The next day I was up and out of bed before the dogs had even opened their eyes. That gave them a bit of a shock. I hurriedly slopped the tinned Pedigree Chum into their bowls, before scorching my mouth as I gulped down a mug of coffee. I was a woman on a mission.

I wasn't due at the West Bridgford branch of the video shop until 10 a.m., in time to start booking back in the

Friday night rentals. It would be a twenty-minute drive on a busy Saturday morning, as the roads were bound to be snarled up with all the shoppers heading for a day in Nottingham. But that still gave me plenty of time to get down to the field in Holme Pierrepont and take a look at this donkey.

Peering out through the kitchen window, I could see my back lawn glistening from an overnight downpour. It was going to be a muddy day. So I tugged on my green welly boots and, as an afterthought, doubled back into the kitchen to grab a carrot from the veg rack. *That donkey deserves a treat after spending all night out in that miserable weather*, I thought, shivering at the morning chill as I unlocked the front door and stepped onto the block-paving driveway.

As I drove the ten-minute journey down to the field, I was surprised to realise I had butterflies in the pit of my stomach. I think it was not knowing what I'd find. I was sure Steve was right, that this mysterious donkey would be fine, but what if he wasn't? What if I was too late? He could be up to his knees in mud, cold and starving. Or, perhaps even worse. I felt the same way I'd done aged seven, telling myself that those little mice needed me to look after them. I felt some silly sense of responsibility for this creature, even though I hadn't set eyes on him yet.

I pulled up on the grassy verge next to the fence, and got my first glimpse of what Steve had seen the night before. It wasn't a donkey, though, it was a mule. To many people, a mule and a donkey would look almost identical. After all, a mule is a hybrid of a male donkey and a female horse, so of course they share lots of physical characteristics. But after two decades of horse riding and hanging around the yard I was fine-tuned to the little giveaways. For one, mules are quite a bit bigger than donkeys. They also have longer, slimmer ears, and a sleek, swishy tail like a horse. I couldn't blame Steve for not spotting the difference, it had been pitch-black when he'd driven by. But in the stark light of day I could tell that this was most definitely a mule, and an unhappy one at that.

The first thing that struck me was the way he was pacing up and down the paddock, swinging his head around wildly. That kind of behaviour is called weaving, and I'd occasionally seen horses do it too. It's a sure sign of boredom or stress. I got out of the car, and pulled my anorak hood up to keep the drizzle off my naturally curly hair. Then I leaned over the fence to get a better look.

It was no wonder the mule was so miserable. He was trudging through the sticky mud all by himself. My heart panged for him. All animals from the equine species thrive on company, and it's not unknown for a lonely horse or pony to give up on life completely. The poor thing must have been bored out of his mind.

The next thing I noticed was that there wasn't even so much as an overhanging tree for him to shelter under. His dark brown coat was absolutely sodden, and his stocky little legs were sinking into a puddle.

It was time to take a closer look. So I hitched my leg up onto the fence and swung myself over into the field. As I landed in the mud with a squelchy thud, the mule immediately turned his head towards me. Even from fifty metres away I could tell he was sizing me up. I didn't want to spook him so for several minutes I just stood there, letting him get used to my presence. He didn't take his eyes off me. Slowly, I inched my hand into my pocket where I'd stashed the big juicy carrot, and held it out towards him.

I could see his nostrils twitching, and his firm gaze didn't waver.

'Come on, you know you want to take a bite,' I said, my voice barely above a whisper. My breath curled in the frosty air as I spoke.

My plan, if you can call it that, was to tempt him over so I could take a closer look at what kind of state he was in. But still he didn't take a single step.

Oh, I see, you want me to make all the effort, I thought,

realising if I wanted us to be friends I'd have to go over to him.

So, as if I was moving in slo-mo, I started creeping across the field, still grasping the carrot in my numb hand. I was willing him to trust me. Slowly, I reached forty metres away, thirty, twenty . . .

Then suddenly, as if a starting pistol had launched a race I didn't know we were in, the mule shattered the silence with a deep bray and began bolting towards me. I dropped the carrot in an instant, and started legging it back towards the fence. My wellies were slipping around in the mud, and dirty splatters were covering my back. I didn't even turn around. The sound of the mule's thundering hooves behind me told me to keep running and running.

I was panting from the effort as I reached the fence and hauled myself back over it. Only then did I glance behind me to see the mule bucking violently. I'd made it just in the nick of time. Ten more seconds and I'd have felt the full force of his muscular hind legs in my backside. It had been a close call.

He finished his antics, and then turned to give me a cool, calm look. I knew exactly what he was thinking. He'd won, and he thought it was hilarious to give me such a fright. But my heart was pounding. I hadn't found it so funny. Then, flippantly, he trotted back to the middle of the field where I'd dropped the carrot. I could have sworn he was mocking me as he snaffled it up and chomped it down, right in front of me.

'You didn't deserve that, you know,' I shouted from the safety of the right side of the fence.

With a flounce, I strode back towards my car. If he wanted to be left alone, he could have it that way. I sat in the driver's seat getting my breath back before starting the ignition. Then, just as I was about to pull away, I caught a glimpse of myself in the rear-view mirror. My hair was frizzy from the rain, where my hood had slipped off as I'd darted back across the field. I had smears of mud across my face, and my cheeks were flushed from having run the fastest I'd run since cross-country in school.

Despite myself, I felt a smile creep across my face. What a shambles. *Just wait until Steve hears about this*, I thought. *He'll be rolling on the floor with laughter.* I'd been feeling so sorry for that poor mule, and this was how he'd repaid me.

I made it to the video shop just in time to start work, and headed straight to the staff loo to clean myself up over the sink. I'd done the best I could with a tissue I'd found in my handbag, but the telltale smears of mud were still there. I didn't fancy trying to explain this one to my mum. I already felt like a right idiot.

'Are you all right to get on with a bit of stocktaking?' my mum asked when I finally reappeared.

'No problem,' I said, brushing the last crumbs of drying mud off my jeans.

I'd got away with it. I spent the rest of the morning holed up in the back room, checking our VHS tapes off on a sheet. But still my mind kept drifting back to that blooming mule. *He didn't look too skinny or mistreated*, I thought to myself. *Just a bit muddy.* I'd managed to get a better look while he was stood there munching away on my carrot, the cheeky git. Still, though, the idea of him there all alone was bothering me.

I wondered whether his field mate had been taken out for a ride, or a trip to the vet's. Perhaps he wasn't really alone. But then again, Steve reckoned he'd been all by himself the night before too. Or maybe he'd just been put in the field as a temporary measure until he went off to a proper home. I tried to make myself concentrate on the task at hand. Those videos wouldn't count themselves.

By the end of my shift, in spite of myself, I'd nearly forgotten how cross I'd been when he tried to boot me over the fence. Instead, I was feeling sorry for him.

*

'Did you meet the donkey then?' Steve asked, as I slumped down on the sofa between him and Jenna, who was snoring away.

'It's a mule actually,' I said, teasing him. 'And he's a proper nasty bugger.'

'Couldn't you tempt him with the carrot? Did he not fancy making friends?' Steve asked.

'Oh, he had the carrot all right,' I said, and started recounting my morning.

Steve was in stitches as I described how I'd leaped over the fence, with seconds to spare. I started giggling too.

'Seriously, though, he wasn't happy by himself. Who do you reckon he belongs to?' I said.

'No idea. I'll ask around, see if we can suss your horrible friend out.'

This time there would be no space to stash the mule away in a cosy box at the bottom of the wardrobe, but I'd already started hatching a rescue plan. There was something about him that had really found a place in my heart. I guess you could say I'd fallen for him. If no one else wanted him, I sure did.

2

Horsing Around

'Hello again, you horrible thing,' I said, with more than a hint of affection.

It was Sunday and, no surprise, I was back down at the field to see the mule. He was still pacing around, just as he had been the day before. However, as a small mercy, the previous night had been a clear one and the mud was starting to dry up. The dirt was flaking off his legs, and he looked scruffier than the last time I'd seen him. I could tell that his mood hadn't improved either, as he fixed me with a stroppy gaze. It was as if he was thinking, *Not you again.*

I wasn't taking any chances this time. There was no way I was getting back in that field. I'd brought backup too, in the form of Steve. If the mule decided to have a kick at us, at least there was only a fifty per cent chance it would be me that his filthy hooves struck.

'I know what you mean, there's something about him,' Steve said thoughtfully, watching him stare us out.

'It's like he's playing hard to get. He's making it as difficult as he can for us to like him, but for some reason that only makes me like him more,' I said.

'I still wish I'd been here yesterday to see you in that field with him,' Steve said, chuckling.

'Yeah, I bet you do. Lob him that carrot then, and we'll go and see what we can find out about him.'

He chucked it over into the field. Then, without taking his suspicious eyes off us, the mule stalked over and crunched it down. He might not have wanted to be our friend, but he certainly wasn't shy about taking food from us. Not that I expected him to have any manners, after what I'd seen the day before.

'Right, let's start at the pub,' Steve said with a grin.

Before long, we were perched at the bar in the Black Lion, with half a lager for me and a pint of bitter for Steve in front of us.

It sounds like a cliché, but the Black Lion really was the hub of the village. It has sadly closed down now, but back then it was the most popular drinking spot around. It was a traditional old inn, with a bar area and a separate lounge. Many a friendship had been made, broken and then mended over a pint in there. And, like any good landlord, Wilf behind the bar always had a handle on the latest comings and goings. It was only sensible that our search for the owner of the mule should start with him. If that happened to mean we'd buy a pint or two first, well, that was just a happy coincidence.

We were halfway through our drinks when a quiet lull at the bar gave us a chance to ask.

'Here, Wilf, I don't suppose you know anything about that mule down in Holme Pierrepont, do you?' Steve asked.

'Hmm, I noticed him a couple of days ago too,' Wilf said, as he wiped down the wooden bar top. 'Not sure who he belongs to, though, if that's what you mean. Why, did you fancy buying him or something?'

Steve laughed, and I felt my cheeks flush. I hadn't mentioned it to Steve yet, but that was exactly what I'd been thinking. Although I had a funny feeling that Steve might have been considering the same too.

'I'm sure someone will know. I'll ask around for you,' the landlord said, before heading off to take some dirty glasses down to the kitchen.

We finished our pints and headed home for the evening, both in quiet contemplation. As my brain whirred, I couldn't help but get ahead of myself. *If we did buy the mule, where would we keep him?* I wondered. Our garden would be no home for him. We had a carefully paved patio area, with a fairly small patch of lawn. Plus, I didn't think our tortoises, Walter and Betty, would appreciate their peace being invaded by that moody animal. But I was sure I'd figure something out. Where there's a will there's always a way.

For the next few days I kept everything crossed that Wilf at the Black Lion would have some news for us. In the meantime, I was checking daily on our mule. I knew he didn't actually belong to me and Steve, but already I was thinking of him as ours. By this point I was satisfied that he didn't need any immediate help. He seemed healthy enough, and he had plenty of grass to eat. He couldn't live on his own forever, though.

Then, one evening Steve popped in at the pub for a quick pint after work with a mate. He came home with a grin on his face, looking ever so pleased with himself.

'I've got a phone number for our mule owner,' he said, waving a scrap of paper. 'Wilf managed to track him down for us. Apparently he does the donkey rides over at a beach in Lincolnshire somewhere.'

I glanced at the kitchen clock. Seven thirty p.m. It certainly wasn't too late to give the bloke a ring.

'Give it here then,' I said, walking over to the corner of the kitchen where the phone was mounted on the wall.

I didn't even pause to think about what I was going to say if the man answered. I was too excited. It felt like an age before a grumpy voice on the other end snapped, 'Hello.'

'Oh, hi. I was wondering about that mule you've got down in Holme Pierrepont. It is yours, isn't it?' I said.

'That miserable sod? Yes, he's mine unfortunately. Why, do you want him?' he replied.

The way he was describing the mule, I immediately knew we were talking about the same one. Surely there couldn't be a second mule as badly tempered as ours. However, I was a bit taken aback. I was expecting to have to use a bit of persuasion to bring up the offer of a sale.

'Well, maybe, are you selling?' I said.

'If you want him, you're welcome to him. Some travellers passing through the area flogged him to me as a perfect seaside donkey. He's ever so placid, they said. Well, I was well and truly conned,' he said.

'Oh?'

'I tried him on the beach, but he was having none of it. He'd have happily killed a child. I was only putting him in that field until I found something else to do with him. He's no use to me,' he said. 'You'll have to pay me, though.'

It seemed almost laughable. Here was a bloke with a

mule he didn't even want, and I was potentially offering him a good home. Still, he wanted me to pay him, and at £250 the price was steep. If anything, he should have been offering to pay me for doing him a favour. I should have told him where to go, and put the phone down. Yet I couldn't give up on my rescue plans at the first hurdle.

'Give me a day or two, and I'll call you back,' I said.

I turned to Steve, who'd been hanging on every word of the phone call.

'It's his, but he wants two hundred and fifty pounds.' I knew we didn't have that kind of money to spare.

'Let's see what we can do then,' Steve said.

In that instant, I knew I wasn't going to have to sell Steve the idea of taking in the mule. He was almost as smitten with the idea as me. But first we had some planning to do.

There wasn't much we could do about the financial situation. The simple fact was that we didn't have £250 to spend. But fortunately, our families were generous. We made a few phone calls, explained the plan, and soon, by begging and borrowing, we had scraped together enough cash. I wrote out a cheque and popped it in the post to the owner, John Murphy, who lived out at Addlethorpe near Skegness.

The next immediate problem was where the mule

would live. I'd already ruled out the garden, and we didn't have any other land. However, I did know a farmer who owned some land in between Radcliffe-on-Trent and Holme Pierrepont and I managed to talk him into letting us put our new mule in with a herd of his cows. That way the mule would have some company, and one more mouth nibbling the grass wouldn't put the farmer out.

We arranged to go and pick up the mule the next Saturday morning. I'd bought a brand-new head collar and a rope, ready for the job. There was just one more thing to sort out. We couldn't keep calling him 'him'. He needed a name. The owner already had that covered, though. When I phoned to double-check the handover arrangements I found out he was called Muffin.

'What other name could there be for a mule?' I said to Steve, laughing.

'Sounds good to me,' Steve agreed.

Neither Steve nor I had ever watched the original BBC children's TV show starring the Muffin the Mule puppet. It ended in the 1950s, so a bit before our time. But we knew the character.

So that Saturday we set off to the field armed with the head collar, a name, and a packet of ginger biscuits. Just because Muffin was now ours didn't mean he'd behave for us. I was ready to use bribes if we had to, and everyone knows that horses love a ginger snap. I was keeping my fingers crossed that our grouchy mule would too.

I took a deep breath for courage, and once again climbed over into the field. Steve and I had a plan. We'd get as close to Muffin as we could, then I'd scatter some chunks of biscuit for him to crunch on. We'd inch closer and closer, offering more biscuits along the way, until Steve could slip the head collar on. Then we'd lead Muffin out of the gate, down the road, and into the cow field where the farmer would be waiting for us. He'd trot off happily to enjoy his new home, and we'd be sitting back at the house with a cuppa and a biscuit before we knew it. It sounded so simple, but of course it didn't prove to be that easy.

We weren't surprised to find that Muffin was still his same old surly self. He fixed us with a mardy glare, and I was ready to make a run for it again. But Steve decided he wasn't going to have any of his nonsense. He started to make his way across to the far side of the field, hiding the head collar behind his back, out of Muffin's view. He hissed at me to follow with the biscuits. My heart was racing as I rustled a couple out of the packet, and threw them towards Muffin.

'I've got some lovely biscuits for you, come on,' I said soothingly.

Muffin looked less than impressed with our arrival. However, he couldn't resist a delicious titbit. He took a few steps forward and crunched down a piece of biscuit in one gulp. Then he gave us a suspicious look, and I could have sworn he was wondering what the catch was. It was like he was thinking, *Why are these awful people giving me such tasty treats?* His belly won over his brain, though, and he came a bit closer to snaffle another ginger snap.

As he went in for the third bit of biscuit, I gave Steve a silent nod. This was our chance. I grabbed another biscuit and waved it in front of me to keep Muffin's attention occupied. Meanwhile, Steve deftly swooped forward with the head collar.

For a moment I thought the job was done. But then Muffin tossed his head away just in the nick of time and let out an almighty ear-shattering bray, before cantering off to the furthest side of the field.

'Bugger, we should have cornered him,' Steve said.

'It's a good job I bought the large packet of biscuits,' I added.

So we headed over to the other side of the field and began the whole performance again. We quickly realised that Muffin was only too happy to eat our biscuits, but he was damn sure we wouldn't get our hands on him.

To cut to the chase, literally, we were stalking that flipping mule around the field for nearly two hours.

Eventually, exhausted and thoroughly fed up, Steve managed to outsmart him. He pulled the head collar on, giving me the rope to hold to make sure we didn't lose him. Muffin realised he'd been captured, and he was furious. He tried to bolt across the field, pulling me along with him. I was holding on to that rope for dear life, shouting at Steve for help. He got his hands on the rope too, and together we managed to tug Muffin over towards the gate.

After a quick breather, we started to lead Muffin down the lane still bucking and making a spectacle of himself. I wasn't strong enough to hold him so Steve took the rope. The last thing we needed was him making a run for it. If we let him go, there wouldn't be enough biscuits in the world to tempt him back. Steve's poor arms were knackered from the effort by the time we made it to Muffin's new home, where the farmer was waiting.

The field was absolutely huge, so there was plenty of room for one more despite the fifty or so cows already in there. The ground was covered with lush grass, and Muffin was tugging at the rope in an effort to get in there to enjoy himself.

'Can you get the gate open?' I said, calling ahead.

'He looks like a lively one,' the farmer said, frowning as he creaked the gate on its hinge. He didn't know the half of it.

'I think he's just excited about making friends,' I said. It was best the farmer was kept in the dark about how much trouble Muffin had already caused us. I'd promised he'd be as good as gold, and I was sure he'd settle down once he was in there with the cows.

Steve whipped off the head collar, and the farmer clicked the metal gate shut as Muffin trotted quite happily off towards the black and white herd. I breathed a sigh of relief. The rescue mission was complete and now I could relax.

We stood making conversation with the farmer, watching to make sure Muffin was happy in his new home. For a few minutes he was. And then, without warning, he let out a tremendous screech. I winced from the noise; I'd never heard anything like it. By the looks of it, neither had the cows. They were completely spooked, and bolted in every direction.

I stood there gawping in shock as Muffin started chasing them around the field. It was like he thought it was a fantastic new game. He was having the time of his life, but the cows were terrified. With no escape route, they started jumping over the hedge into the road, and running away in both directions.

My stupor was interrupted as the farmer began shouting filthy obscenities about our Muffin.

'You don't want to know what I'm going to do with

that sodding thing when I get my hands on him! Do something! Get him out of there, and move him into the next field! My sheep will show him he's not the boss!' he yelled, before hotfooting it down the lane after his herd.

The cows were long gone, and Steve and I were totally lost for words. Meanwhile, Muffin was still tormenting the few cows that were left in the field.

'Well, that didn't go to plan,' I said, cringing with embarrassment at the chaos we'd caused.

'I thought you said mules like to make friends? In fact, isn't that why we've just shelled out two hundred and fifty pounds for him?' Steve said.

'Obviously not this one,' I replied. I didn't know what else to say. I was completely dumbfounded. Sure, Muffin hadn't exactly taken to me or Steve. But still, I hadn't expected this.

We climbed over the fence, and I groped in my pocket to find the couple of ginger biscuits we had left. I had this overwhelming sense of doom. It was like a bad déjà vu. Except we really had been here before, just half an hour earlier. I sighed as I realised I wouldn't be enjoying that much-needed hot cup of coffee any time soon.

An hour later, we'd finally managed to move Muffin to his second new home of the day. He'd been having so much fun with the cows that he wasn't going to be caught again without a fight. I could barely watch as we set him free among the sheep in the next field, keeping my fingers, toes and everything else crossed that we wouldn't have a repeat of his earlier antics. Thankfully, he seemed much less interested in playing with the sheep. They didn't appear pleased to see him, and gave him a wide berth. He let them be as he lowered his head and started munching on the grass.

'Thank God for that. I don't know what we'd have done with Muffin if he'd upset the sheep too,' I said.

'Let's just hope they don't take any of his nonsense,' Steve said, glancing up and down the lane. 'Shall we get out of here before the farmer comes back?'

'I doubt he's calmed down yet. Good plan,' I agreed.

And so, with one final glance to make sure Muffin was behaving himself, we made our escape even faster than those cows had sprinted down the lane.

By the time we eventually got home it was late afternoon. Forgetting about the coffee, I reached for a large wine glass. After what we'd just been through I figured I deserved it. My arms ached from the strain of trying to keep hold of Muffin on the end of that rope, my coat pockets were filled with crumbs, and I looked even more of a state than I had after our first encounter.

However, there wasn't a single ounce of regret. I couldn't deny Muffin had been a huge pain in the bum, and I had a funny feeling he'd carry on being one too. But I knew that rescuing him was not only the right thing to do, but something that I really wanted to do. His scruffy brown coat was the exact shade of chocolate cake, and his moody expression had a certain charm to it. He might not like me yet, but I was determined that would change. I'd win him over whatever it took. And, in the meantime, at least he had an abundance of grass and some company to enjoy.

Before meeting Muffin I certainly never had any ambition to own a mule or a donkey, or anything like that. I was quite happy with my domestic pets. It sounds like a silly thing to say but having Muffin in my life immediately felt like a natural fit, as if something had been missing before. I felt excited.

The next day I drove to pick up some hay and a huge bag of carrots, and wedged them into the car boot. I was a bit nervous about heading over to see Muffin, not really knowing what I'd arrive to. I wouldn't have been surprised to find him in the field all on his own, having chased the sheep away too. If that was the case, I'd never be able to face the farmer again. But, to my relief, I drove up to a scene of domestic bliss. Muffin was calmly minding his own business and the sheep were minding theirs.

I shook some of the hay into a corner of the field for him to enjoy, and popped a couple of carrots on top too. Muffin barely even registered that I was there. This was progress from the day before, when his glare had been almost murderous. I decided I would rather he ignore me than detest the very sight of me. These small steps were still steps in the right direction. Perhaps this arrangement would work out after all.

3

Fresh Beginnings

Muffin's domestic bliss lasted exactly one week. I'd been down to check on him at least twice every day, morning and evening, with another quick visit to say hello if I could fit one in. My heart had filled with pride to see him happily nibbling on the grass and prancing around. He seemed calmer.

Then early one evening the phone rang.

'Tracy, you need to do something about this donkey. I'm not having him anymore,' said a grouchy voice, without as much as a hello. It was the farmer, and he wasn't pleased with me.

'Why, what's happened?' I asked innocently. A swarm of terrible scenarios started rushing through my mind. Had Muffin escaped? Maybe his friendship with the sheep was over and he'd chased them out of the field too?

'He's been biting at my ewes. They hate him. You need to find him somewhere else to go,' the farmer said.

I sighed. There was no point in arguing; his mind was made up and Muffin had outstayed his welcome.

'I'll sort it out as soon as I can. I'm sorry again about your cows too. Are they all all right?' I asked.

'They're fine now. It took me two days to round them all up, though. Plus, there are the apologies I still need to make to everyone whose garden got trampled in the process,' he said.

I could have sworn I heard a hint of a chuckle in the farmer's voice. With relief, I realised I hadn't burnt all my bridges with him – yet. However, I needed Muffin to stay out of trouble until we found him a new home.

That very evening Steve and I started phoning around everyone we knew who owned land, keeping our fingers crossed someone would have a little bit of spare space. But we drew a blank. Suddenly our garden was looking like a potential option after all. I couldn't bear to think of the damage that mule would do to our perfectly preened lawn, not to mention what the neighbours would say to his racket. *There must be something we can do*, I thought, dreading the complaints from next door already.

Over the next few days, we used our evenings to drive around the village on the lookout for the smallest sliver of derelict land. Eventually we hit the jackpot. We pulled up next to a field that backed on to the railway line, not far from where the River Trent ran. It was filled with what I can only describe as rubbish. The ground was strewn with bin liners, empty drink cans and debris. There was even a burned-out car in the corner.

But underneath the chaos I could see shoots of green grass sprouting through. Perfect for a mule. The field was a good size too, and its location in Island Lane was only a ten-minute walk from home. From the state of it, I was almost certain it wasn't being used.

'What do you reckon? I think this could work,' I said to Steve.

'It's a wreck but your Muffin needs somewhere, I suppose.'

It wasn't clear who owned the area, but as it backed on to the railway I decided that British Rail would be a good place to start. Sure enough, after enquiries had been made, it was determined that the field did belong to them, and they were happy to rent it to me. It was pricey, at just over £1,000 a year, but I was desperate. There was only one condition – I'd have to clear it out myself.

After calling the farmer to tell him the good news we set about making Muffin's new home fit for purpose. With the promise of a couple of pints down at the Black Lion, we roped in some friends to give us a hand in clearing half of the area and re-fencing around the edge.

Before long, Muffin was safely enclosed once more. I was sad to see he'd started weaving again, tossing his head around with boredom. But I was already putting a plan in place to find him some proper friends. I just hoped that this time he'd make a bit more effort himself.

I saw an advert in the local paper, the *Nottingham Evening Post*, looking for people who would be happy to give a Skegness beach donkey a home just for the winter. I learned that during the summer they stayed in an open field near the beach. But as the colder and wetter weather drew in, the donkeys needed somewhere with a bit more shelter. And, to put it bluntly, most of the owners were too tight to pay for that kind of accommodation. The donkeys didn't work in the winter, so they weren't earning their keep. Instead, the owners would appeal to the generosity of the public to keep them warm and fed until spring came around again. It was just the way it had always been done.

I called the number at the bottom of the ad, and agreed to give two beach donkeys a home for the winter. Muffin hadn't liked the cows, and he hadn't really taken to the sheep either. Perhaps one of his own kind would be more up his street. In the meantime, we started work on a shack at the edge of the field to provide a bit of shelter. Then, come September, Noddy and Linda arrived in the back of a trailer. Linda was a steady, sensible sort of character, with perfect manners. Noddy was a little bit more of a handful. I wasn't surprised; his owner had warned me he had a habit of nodding his head until the kids fell off his back. But compared to Muffin, he was an angel.

At this point I didn't really stop to reflect on how the situation had already started to escalate. I'd decided to save one donkey, almost on a bit of a whim. And then there I was with three in my care. Instead, I was excited. I was determined to crack Muffin's miserable exterior and I felt sure that this would do the trick.

At first, he point-blank ignored Noddy and Linda. They stuck to one side of the field, and he kept firmly to the other. Still, it was better than a repeat performance of the debacle with the cows. However, within a fortnight the two factions had begun to warm to each other. Linda would tentatively snuffle over towards Muffin, with Noddy following behind. Muffin would tolerate them invading his space. Gradually, over time, a bond formed and soon they were even grooming each other, scratching their teeth along each other's necks. Maybe Muffin wasn't such a grumpy sod at heart after all.

As all three donkeys settled in to their new surroundings, word soon got around the village about the new residents. Often I'd be down at the field scooping donkey dung onto a spade when a familiar face would pop by to ask whether they could give my furry friends a treat. The donkeys actually enjoyed the attention. Even Muffin would happily stand there for a child to stroke his nose, as long as there was a carrot coming his way. He was a totally reformed character.

The donkeys' growing popularity also had another, more unexpected, effect. People had started to give me a call whenever they spotted a donkey living in unsuitable conditions. I don't know what they thought I'd be able to do about it. I was certainly no expert. But just as I'd been unable to shake the thought of Muffin living unhappily alone, every donkey I heard about found a place in my heart. There was plenty of space in the field, and looking after Muffin and his two pals was proving no trouble. How could I refuse to help any other donkey in need?

By the time Linda and Noddy were picked up for work again in the summer, I'd taken in another two donkeys – Martin and Charlie. Former beach donkey Martin had been ditched by his exasperated owner for taking the children down to sea but refusing to bring them back again. Charlie's story was even sadder, as he'd been abandoned in a lonely paddock in Chapel St Leonards near Skegness with no food or water. By some miracle, he'd escaped without any serious health problems, but he was incredibly thin and very aggressive. I spent months taming his temper and feeding him up. Fortunately, once he'd been castrated he calmed down, but it still didn't stop me having sleepless nights over him. He was the first donkey to need such intensive rehabilitation, and I was determined not to let him down. I'd never intended to start a sanctuary for old, unwanted and mistreated donkeys, but before I knew it that seemed to have happened. It snowballed, despite the sensible side of my brain telling me that my hands were full enough.

Soon we'd rented a second field on the opposite side of the road, and five donkeys became eight, ten, twenty . . . Linda and Noddy joined us permanently and even the RSPCA shelter on the outskirts of the village had started putting people in touch with me. Every time I got a call I'd borrow a horsebox and set off to pick up another rescue case, travelling across the whole of the Midlands and sometimes even further afield. I'd find them through tip-offs from slaughterhouse workers, customers at cattle markets, and concerned members of the public.

I was still holding down the job at the video shop, but looking after my rescue cases was taking up every spare moment I had. Steve and I used to love travelling to Portugal at least twice a year. We'd lap up the sunshine and enjoy the scenery of the Monchique mountains in the south. But from the day we took in Muffin, there was no time or money for anything as frivolous as a holiday. Even pints at the Black Lion had become a rare indulgence. Instead, knackered from hefting bales of hay and hammering fence posts into the ground, I preferred to wash off the mud and climb straight into bed. I soon realised I'd made a huge commitment to these donkeys. But if I didn't look after them, who else would?

I can't say that launching the donkey sanctuary was easy. It was exhausting, expensive, and time consuming. But despite that, it honestly made me happier than I'd been in years. Back when I'd worked in the hairdresser's, I'd known by the end of my first day that it wasn't really for me. I'd enjoyed working in the jewellery shops but knew it wasn't something I wanted to do for the rest of my life. Even working in my parents' video stores was just a stopgap. They'd needed an extra pair of hands and, at the end of the day, a job was a job. But getting up in the morning to take care of my donkeys gave me such a sense of fulfilment. Not a single day went by that didn't make me smile.

Before I knew it a few years had passed, the two fields were filled with donkeys under my care and I felt happier than I ever had. Muffin still loved giving me the run-around, so not much had changed there. I'd wasted many an hour chasing him for the farrier to check over his hooves or so I could give his muddy legs a brush down. He liked to remind me that he thought he was the boss, as if he owed the place. But one afternoon I noticed he wasn't his usual cheeky self. Instead of coming straight to the gate to see what treats I'd brought him, he hovered at the back of the field. Even when I shook some hay out, he didn't dash over. I watched as he walked gingerly through the grass, wincing at the pain his back legs were causing him. They were so stiff.

I got in touch with the vet immediately, who by this time was no stranger to us. Matthew Barlow from the Chine House Veterinary Hospital in Sileby, Leicestershire, really was a miracle worker. He'd been with us since the beginning, from the day he handed me a worming tablet for Muffin and gave him a tetanus shot. He understood that I was ready to go above and beyond to save a donkey, when others might take one look at the state I found them in and declare them a lost cause. That's why I trusted his judgement. He would always be honest with me, and do everything he could to find a solution.

Matthew drove straight over to see Muffin and I explained that I thought he must have injured himself or strained a muscle. Then Matthew leaped over the fence and cornered Muffin for a thorough examination. I watched as he soothingly ran his hands over Muffin's hind quarters, feeling for a problem.

'His legs seem fine. I don't think that's the issue. He's actually got an undescended testicle – we call it a "rig". It means one of his testicles is still up in his abdomen and I think that might be what's causing the pain,' Matthew said.

'Is it dangerous?' I asked, fearing the worst.

'It's not as rare as you might think. He'll need surgery but after that he should be fine. It explains his bad temper, though. Too much testosterone,' he said, with a knowing smile.

I felt relieved. Muffin might have landed me with another expensive vet bill, but at least he'd recover. So I arranged with Matthew that I'd bring Muffin over to the operating centre the next day. He would be castrated, or gelded as it is referred to in the equine world.

By now we had our own shiny blue Ifor Williams double horsebox, which had been donated by the local Co-op as part of their Community Dividend scheme. They'd asked me what I needed, and I'd told them I was desperate for some hay. But they decided that they wanted to donate something that they could put their name on. The trailer was worth around £3,000, and would save me the cost of hiring one every time I needed to take one of the donkeys off to the vet's. In the years to come it proved to be an invaluable asset.

So on the morning of Muffin's operation I loaded him into our horsebox and then gave him a little cuddle as I dropped him off.

'Don't worry, you'll be right as rain soon. Be good for the vet,' I said, handing him over to a kind-looking veterinary nurse.

'We'll take good care of him. You'll get a phone call later when he's ready to be picked up,' she said, taking the rope from me.

'He's a bit of a lively one so . . . erm . . . be careful,' I added, almost sheepishly. Muffin had calmed down considerably since I'd first taken him in but I still wouldn't have put it past him to cause a ruckus if he felt so inclined. I didn't fancy a long list of pricey repairs being added to my vet bill too.

For the rest of the day Muffin wasn't far from my mind. I knew Matthew would be looking after him but still I couldn't help but worry. I imagine it's like being a parent with a poorly child. You feel helpless. I spent the morning clock-watching, waiting for the call to pick up my mule.

Then the phone rang. Steve got to the kitchen first and picked it up, while I hovered in the doorway waiting for the nod to grab my keys and head back to Sileby.

But then a serious expression fell over Steve's face. He frowned as he listened to what the vet had to say.

'If you think that's best, then that's what you should do. You know we trust you, Matthew,' he said.

I had to stop myself from grabbing the phone out of Steve's hands, desperate to find out what was going on. I could tell it wasn't good news. Steve put down the phone, and shook his head sadly.

'Matthew got him on the operating table, but then he found that Muffin's testicle has turned cancerous. The tumour's big, and there's nothing he can do,' Steve said.

'There's always something! People are cured of cancer all the time, so why not a mule?' I cried.

'I'm afraid not,' Steve said. 'Matthew told me it would be kindest to put Muffin to sleep while he's still under general anaesthetic. You heard me, I told him we'd trust his judgement.'

Saying I was devastated doesn't do it justice. Muffin was the founding member of my donkey sanctuary, and I hadn't lost a rescue case yet. It didn't seem real. He'd gone to the vet's for a routine op and now I was being told he wasn't coming home again. I couldn't even say goodbye.

I spent the rest of the day in floods of tears. There was nothing Steve could say to comfort me, as he was just as upset as I was. I felt guilty for not realising there was something wrong with Muffin before, even though Matthew had already assured me I couldn't have known. I felt like a failure. I was supposed to have rescued Muffin so he could enjoy a long and happy life. Instead, it had been cut so tragically short.

We paid to have Muffin cremated and a week later we received his ashes. I cried as I scattered them across his field, remembering him standing there just days before. He'd been so happy living with us, even if he hadn't always shown it. It hurt that he hadn't been able to enjoy his new life for longer.

I pulled myself together for the sake of the rest of the donkeys. They still needed me. But Muffin's death clouded my head for a long time after that. It was the first taste of the heartbreak that running a donkey sanctuary would bring. I'd never really considered the fact that, of course, they wouldn't live forever. We'd nursed so many back from the brink when they came to us malnourished and mistreated that they seemed almost invincible. And I certainly never expected that Muffin would be the first that we'd lose. It was almost unbearably unfair.

Muffin's death left a big hole not just in my life, but among the donkeys' too. Naturally, he'd been the boss of his field and they didn't seem to know what to do with themselves without him. The younger males started squabbling as the pecking order was re-established. It was behaviour I hadn't seen before, and for the next fortnight I had sleepless nights worrying over whether we'd ever recover from losing Muffin. Thankfully, it wasn't long before things calmed down.

No sooner had we settled back into a routine when life threw us another curveball. Up until now, the admin of getting a sanctuary off the ground had been smooth. We'd applied for planning permission for a small stable, which had been approved. The financial side of things was ticking along too. People had started to donate money and food for the donkeys and, with the help of a few keen fund-raisers, we just about made ends meet. On the whole, the village loved having the donkey sanctuary on its doorstep. That's except for one particular neighbour.

First it was the noise of the donkeys braying. Next it was the smell of their manure. Then it was the regular trickle of visitors coming to see the donkeys. I tried to hold my tongue and meet each complaint with an apology and a suggestion of how we might be able to put things right. Soon, though, the situation became infuriating. Why shouldn't you expect the sounds and smells of animals in the countryside? And as for the visitors, we weren't even officially open to the public. People just liked to pop by, or they'd stop for a chat as they walked their dogs. I couldn't stop them, especially when they were happy to donate much-needed cash in return.

Soon things had escalated and Nottinghamshire County Council became involved. I wasn't exactly delighted at the idea of them butting their noses in, but I was at a loss as to what I could do to appease the main complainer. I got a letter to inform us that the county council would be considering whether to put restrictions on what we could and couldn't do. However, first it would be discussed by Radcliffe-on-Trent Parish Council, to see what the local consensus was.

The parish council invited me and Steve along to the public meeting. This made me nervous. Up until this point, the donkey sanctuary and its future had been in my hands. Now, it was being taken out of my control. Suddenly I was being asked to justify what I was doing. Surely it was obvious why I was spending day and night and every penny in my purse on the sanctuary? It was for the donkeys.

We arrived at the village hall for the meeting to scenes of absolute chaos. We wanted to get there early to settle our nerves, ahead of the 7.30 p.m. start. It seemed like the rest of the village had had the same idea too. People were spilling out of the door. But when they saw that we'd arrived they made way for us to get through.

'We'll tell them we love the donkeys,' one woman said, stepping back for me to squeeze by.

'We're here to support you,' another said.

I was gobsmacked as I realised that all of these people were there to stick up for the donkeys. I knew people didn't mind us being there, although I presumed it was because we were tucked out of the way, away from the main part of the village. But I never appreciated we had so much support. It was completely heart-warming.

We eventually found ourselves a seat in the public area of the meeting room, with people packed in around us. There was standing room only at the back. The parish councillors looked a bit bemused as they called the room to order to start the meeting. I don't think there was much in the history of Radcliffe-on-Trent that had ever caused such a stir. I listened as the councillors outlined the purpose of the meeting, my blood boiling as they listed the complaints made against us. Sure, they all stemmed from one individual, but it was still hard to hear.

Steve and I weren't allowed to have our say, but it was clear that the councillors had done their research. They talked about how parents from the village loved taking their children down to visit, and how local business owners said that the donkey sanctuary had really put the village on the map.

My heart was in my mouth as the parish councillors started to discuss what their response to the county council would be. Then they held a vote, which resulted in them agreeing to send a letter supporting us. I couldn't stop myself from grinning. There was still a battle to be done – the final decision was in the hands of the county council. But having such an amazing show of support felt like a victory.

In the days that followed, donations were being made left, right and centre, and it seemed that we had more visitors popping by than ever. *That will please our complainer*, I thought, laughing to myself as I imagined him realising he'd made us more popular than we had been in the first place. People had even begun writing in to the local paper to support us.

The sanctuary is a credit to Tracy and to Radcliffe, one wrote. *Many of the people who complain do not help any charity at all, so they should just shut up and let us get on with it!* wrote another.

It felt like we were living in limbo until the county council made their decision. Then one morning an official-looking letter dropped through the letterbox.

'I think this is it, Steve,' I said, my hands trembling slightly as I scooped it up from the doormat.

'Let's have a look then. We might as well face the music,' he said.

I tore open the envelope, and my heart sank. I turned straight to the long list of conditions that the council had decided to put on the sanctuary. We were strictly forbidden from hosting members of the public, apart from one single open day per year. Plus, the council had decided that the arbitrary figure of twenty donkeys was enough. We weren't allowed to keep more than that.

'This is going to be impossible,' I said to Steve, my head in my hands.

Public donations would soon dry up if we had to ban people from seeing the donkeys. And as we already had nineteen donkeys at that time, how could I turn away all but one?

'We'll find a way to manage, don't worry,' Steve said.

I could tell he was being optimistic for my benefit. He was bitterly disappointed too.

In the weeks that followed we tried to put the council's decision behind us. There was nothing we could do about it, we'd have to accept it. All our local supporters couldn't have been more sympathetic. Meanwhile, we carried on caring for our donkeys. Admittedly our fields might have looked a bit fuller than the council would have liked, but the ruling only mentioned donkeys. They hadn't thought to put a restriction on mules or horses.

4

New Neighbours

My head pounded as I sat at the kitchen table poring over our bank accounts. Money was draining out to the vet, our feed supplier, the farrier, the equine dentist . . . What was giving me a headache was the lack of money coming in. I was still working all hours in the video stores, and Steve was still travelling up and down the country as a printer-engineer. We were scrimping and saving every penny that we could. But that wasn't enough. Just as we'd feared, some people lost interest when we had to tell them that they weren't allowed to come and cuddle our donkeys. And as the visitors dried up, so did our cash supply.

'We can't go on like this, Steve,' I said. 'If we run out of money, we'll cope, but what about the donkeys?'

'Maybe we should have another look at moving? I don't want to any more than you do, but I don't think we'll have a choice soon,' he said.

We'd been talking about finding another location for the sanctuary ever since the county council had laid down the law. It always came back to the same sticking point, though. We loved living in Radcliffe-on-Trent, and the vast majority of the village loved having us there. It didn't seem fair that we should have to uproot our lives. But still, our financial situation was doomed. We felt cornered, as if the decision had been taken out of our hands.

So, with much sadness, we put our home on the market and started scanning through the land advertised for sale in the local newspapers. Firstly, we needed more space, at least a few acres. Secondly, the location had to be remote. We didn't want to move just to be lumbered with a new set of nuisance neighbours. Finding a new home for us wasn't a priority. We were prepared to live in a caravan if it meant that the donkeys would be happy. But everywhere we found was so expensive. We'd been well and truly priced out of the area.

Then one evening Steve came home from work grinning from ear to ear. He'd recently changed his career, but he was still away from home just as much as ever. He'd set himself up as a self-employed plant machinery dealer, buying and selling construction vehicles and all sorts.

'I was on my way back from Skegness, and there was

a flipping huge diversion in place. It was emergency roadworks or something, I reckon. Anyway, it took me down all these country roads,' he told me.

'Oh right,' I said, barely glancing up from the sink where I was peeling the spuds for tea. I didn't see why roadworks would have put my husband in such a good mood.

'Well, anyway, I think I've found us a house,' he said.

'Really?' I dropped the potato peeler with a clatter.

'Seriously. I saw a "for sale" sign outside a derelict farmhouse, so I pulled over to have a look. It's got loads of land, perfect for what we need. And there's nothing but fields and fields all around, so no more nosy parkers interfering.'

'And where did you say this was?' I asked, wondering how we hadn't already noticed it in the property ads.

'This is the only catch. It's over in Lincolnshire, seventy miles or so, I reckon,' Steve said. 'I jotted down the agent's number, so I'll give them a call in the morning. It can't hurt to find out a bit more about it, can it?'

I murmured that I agreed. Already my head was in the clouds, imagining fields filled with each and every donkey that could possibly need a new home. No more stupid rules, no more complaints. But still, seventy miles was a big move.

I sternly told myself not to get too excited. We'd

already had a look at lots of land, and nothing so far had worked out. Then, in the morning, Steve made the call.

'We'd love to show you round. When are you available?' the estate agent asked him, leaping at the chance for a potential sale. 'There's one tiny issue I need you to be aware of, though. Nothing at all to worry about, but the farmhouse currently has squatters living there.'

'Oh, well, erm . . .' Steve said, already imagining an expensive legal battle that we certainly couldn't afford.

'It's all being taken care of by the current owner; we'll have an eviction order sorted in no time at all,' she breezed, like it was no big deal. 'Oh, and the house has no running water. So, how about we take a look tomorrow?'

I was sold on the house from the moment we pulled up outside. Steve hadn't been exaggerating – there was no shortage of space. I barely even registered the wreck of the farmhouse by the road. Instead, I strode straight past into the open countryside behind.

'So, how much of this land would be ours?' I asked the estate agent.

The old farm was on the edge of Huttoft, a small village not far from the town of Alford. It sat just two miles from the coast, between Skegness and Mablethorpe.

If I could have scooped it up and moved it all to the edge of Radcliffe-on-Trent, I would have. But distance aside, it was perfect.

'We could separate all of this into paddocks, and then build some stable blocks just slightly away from the house,' I said, turning to Steve with a smile twitching at my lips.

'There's a lot of work to be done.' He was frowning at the well in the garden. 'So that's our water supply then?' he asked, turning to the estate agent.

'Yep, that's it,' she said with a tight smile. 'But as you'd be sorting out an electricity supply anyway, getting the house plumbed in wouldn't cause too much disruption.'

'It hasn't got electricity either?' Steve asked.

'Not yet. The house has got lots of potential, though. Heaps of character,' she blagged. Apparently the previous owner had inherited the house, and had tried to rent it out without doing any modernisation.

Eventually Steve tore me away from planning the donkeys' new home to have a look at what could end up being ours. I poked my head around the back door, taking in the gloomy, dark mess inside. *Potential is about all this farmhouse does have*, I thought to myself. The floors were black, the walls were covered in graffiti and the staircase had been completely burned-out in a fire.

The squatters were nowhere to be seen, but the agent whispered that they were still around somewhere.

'Looks good to me,' I shrugged.

Steve rolled his eyes. There was plenty of room for my rescue cases, and that was all that mattered.

We couldn't put in an offer on the farmhouse right away. First we needed to check that the district council would give us permission to set up the sanctuary. We had to apply to change the use of the land from agriculture, as well as putting in for planning permission for our stable block. No one else seemed remotely interested in snapping up the property but I was still worried that someone would get there first. The next few weeks dragged. In the meantime, we sold our house to a cash buyer and spent the next eight weeks squeezed in with my mum and stepdad in Radcliffe-on-Trent.

Eventually, the squatters left, East Lindsey District Council gave us the green light, and the farmhouse was ours. It was a truly bittersweet moment, as new beginnings always are. I was excited for the future, but having to say goodbye to our friends from the village was harder than I expected. It had been our home for ten years.

On moving day, all hands came on deck to help us transport our menagerie across two counties. One of my friends had a huge cattle transporter, so the plan was to fit most of the donkeys in that. We'd also borrowed several horseboxes to take the rest of the animals over in. We were going to set off in a convoy, before meeting more friends who were already waiting at the other end to help with the unloading. It sounded so simple but, as I'd come to learn, when you work with animals anything can happen.

There's a famous saying about being as stubborn as a mule. Muffin himself had shown that there was truth in that. But actually it wasn't any of our donkeys or mules that caused a fuss this time around. One by one they quite happily trotted into the transporter. All I had to do was wave a couple of ginger biscuits in front of their noses and they did exactly what I wanted them to. Phase one was complete.

Then we started to load Senna into a horsebox. He was a retired racehorse once known as Formula One, who'd been a 200/1 chance in the sham that was the 1993 Grand National. The race began with a false start and, after all the jockeys had been regathered, Formula One was raring to go. But another false start scuppered the second attempt too, and jockey Richard Dunwoody even ended up with the starting tape caught around his neck. The official was waving the foul flag but, totally oblivious, most of the riders set off around the course regardless. Meanwhile, Formula One languished by the start line ready for a third restart. There was an uproar when the officials declared the whole race was void and that there wouldn't be another run. It became known as 'the Grand National that never was', and you can still watch the farce on YouTube.

Formula One came to us several years later, after his retirement from racing. He was still fit to ride, and I was on the lookout for a horse I could saddle up. He wasn't really a rescue case, more of a personal project. He had a race name, Formula One, but we weren't sure what his stable name was. It seemed only fitting to name him after the respected Formula One champion Ayrton Senna.

Senna fitted in with the donkeys perfectly. Although he towered above them, they became best of friends. On moving day, that was precisely the problem. He'd seen all his donkey mates loaded into the transporter, and he was convinced they were being taken away from him. So he mounted a protest and decided there was no way he'd be moved until the donkeys were returned.

'Come on, Senna, you've been in and out of horse-boxes all your life,' I said, growing frustrated as he refused to take a single step forward.

I waved a juicy carrot around like a prat, before draping a hood over his face. I thought I could trick him into being led into the horsebox. But he was as still as a statue. Next I took the hood off and tried using a lunge line to lead him forwards. He looked at me with silent determination. He wasn't going anywhere until he got his donkeys back.

For two hours there was a tense stand-off. I sent the donkeys on ahead, while I tried everything I could to get Senna aboard.

'Am I going to have to saddle you up and ride you there?' I asked him, exasperated. I was only half joking. One way or another I needed Senna to play ball.

It became a battle of wills. I could tell Senna was getting bored, and I certainly was too. It was a case of which of us would give up first. I was determined it wasn't going to be me. I seized upon his moment of weakness, and fished the carrot out of my coat pocket again.

'This is yours, but you know what you've got to do first,' I said, stepping back towards the horsebox.

He cracked and begrudgingly stepped up the ramp and into the container. I swung the doors shut behind him, before he could change his mind. Two hours behind schedule and finally we set off for pastures new.

The animals were settled in their new enclosures, and I was sure that soon they'd have forgotten their Island Lane home. The same couldn't be said for me and Steve.

We'd spent so many hours setting up the paddocks and tending to the land that we'd completely neglected to get the farmhouse ready for our arrival.

The squatters had left the place in a total mess. There were piles of rubbish scattered throughout and, huddled in a blanket, I didn't understand how they could have made the place their home. It was freezing cold, gloomy and grim. We cleared one of the downstairs rooms and moved in there with an old mattress, a table, a couple of chairs and a little two-ring camping stove It was worlds away from the comfort of our old home. The things I put myself through for those blooming donkeys.

For the next few months we lived in total squalor, determined to get the stables finished for the donkeys before the weather turned really cold. God knows how many cans of beans we got through, heated on the gas stove for tea. We didn't have much spare time to explore the village, not that there was much to explore. Just a small school, a church, a petrol garage and a pub. However, the locals certainly made us feel very welcome. The landlord at the Axe and Cleaver always greeted us warmly on the rare occasion we found time for a swift pint, and the bloke who ran the garage would ask us how we were getting on when we popped in to fill up the tank.

We were really grateful, as Huttoft was only a small

place in the middle of miles of farmland. We wanted the peace and quiet but, being right on the edge of the village, we could have felt quite isolated. However, our old friends Sue and Brian from Radcliffe-on-Trent had actually moved to the area not long before we did. That was a huge blessing – they did a lot of groundwork for us by introducing us to all the friends they'd made, and soon people were offering to wash our clothes and cook hot food for us. Before long we felt part of the community.

After six months, we decided enough was enough. I was sick of sleeping in layers and layers of clothes, so we relented and borrowed a touring caravan to sleep in. Then eventually, over the next year, our attention turned to bringing the farmhouse up to scratch.

The building was over one hundred years old, and it had never been modernised. It even had an outside loo. Some people would have run a mile, but Steve's pretty handy and he loves a project. Soon the place had been completely gutted and a new roof was put on. Then, bit by bit, the inside was rebuilt. It needed a new staircase, flooring, windows, plasterwork, everything really. I loved watching our home come together.

For the most part, I adored the total peace and quiet that came with living in the heart of the countryside.

There wasn't even as much as a street light to ruin our sense of absolute isolation. I found that out to my cost.

Jenna, Rumpole and Ben had made the move with us, and had settled in just as well as the donkeys. Then one evening I opened the caravan door to take them out for one last wee before bed. I took a torch and we set off on our regular route around the fields.

We got halfway round when the torch beam started to flicker.

'Bugger,' I said, giving it a firm shake.

By the time I'd taken another few steps the light had given up completely. As I looked up to get my bearings before heading back to the house, I realised it was pitch-black. I couldn't even see my hand in front of my face, let alone what I'd stumble across if I started to walk forwards. There was no sign of the light from the caravan so I didn't even know which direction to head in.

My heart began pounding with panic, and I crouched so I could grab the dogs for comfort. I felt alone and terrified.

'Right, we need to find our way home now,' I said, receiving a lick on my hand from one of them in return.

I stood completely still for the next few minutes, desperately trying to work out which direction I'd been heading in. Had I turned around when the torch gave out? Which field was I even in?

Then, with a shudder, I convinced myself that the best plan was to start walking. So I edged over to where I thought the fence was and felt an immense sense of relief when my hand touched upon the rough wood. I began feeling my way down, or up, the field, calling for the dogs to follow me. I tentatively put one foot in front of the other, unable to see what I was about to step on.

Inch by inch, we made our way through the field until I spotted a chink of light in the distance. It was the caravan – or at least it was something. I picked up my pace and, as I pushed open the caravan door, I realised I was shaking.

'Where did you get to? I was about to come out to look for you,' Steve said.

'Don't ask. That bloody torch gave up on me, and I got lost,' I said. 'I couldn't see a thing.'

It sounds like a silly thing for a grown woman to admit, but I'd been genuinely scared by the experience. For the next few weeks I insisted that we sleep with the light on. I'd realised just how isolated we were.

As soon as the place was looking presentable, we opened our gates to the public. We'd never intended to launch a tourist attraction, but then again I'd never really planned to open a donkey sanctuary either. One thing had led to another, and the council's ruling in Radcliffe-on-Trent had proven just how much we relied on public support, and public money.

We decided to stick with our original name – the Radcliffe Donkey Sanctuary. After all, that was where it had all started. I got some fliers printed off and started to distribute them around the campsites and caravan parks up and down the coast. Every school holiday the seaside resorts would be flooded with families, and I decided to capitalise on this. Kids love animals, and I thought maybe some of the mums would chuck us a couple of quid for keeping them occupied for a while.

We soon proved to be one of the most popular attractions in the area. I'm not really a people person, but I couldn't deny I was delighted to see how many visitors would pull up in our car park each day. We decided not to charge an entrance fee. Instead, people could pop their loose change into one of the donation buckets dotted around the place. Some people would come back day after day for their entire holiday, I was sure this would help us get back onto a solid financial footing.

But when, at the end of each day, I emptied out the buckets, the numbers didn't stack up. Some days there would be little more than a handful of coppers in there, even though the sanctuary had been flooded with screaming children all afternoon. I started to count the number of visitors coming through the gates and worked out that the average donation was just five pence per head. It was pitiful. I didn't want to put a price on my donkeys, but surely they were worth more than that?

I began plotting ways to generate more money. Just hoping that people would donate out of goodwill clearly wasn't working. So I started inviting children to adopt any of the donkeys that took their fancy. For just twenty pounds a year, they'd get to support their chosen donkey and they'd receive a nice shiny certificate in return. Twenty pounds doesn't really go that far. The running costs of the sanctuary were in the tens of thousands, and that was just to keep our heads above water. We didn't make a profit, but then again we weren't actually aiming to.

Then I began offering visitors the chance to feed the donkeys. They could pay fifty pence for a little bucket filled to the brim with carrots. Nearly everyone took up this opportunity, with the aim of luring the donkeys over for a stroke and a funny photo. Of course, I kept a close eye on how much the donkeys were being fed. Soon we bought a big barbecue and started selling burgers and sausages for the visitors too.

For the first time, we had a steady stream of cash coming in to the sanctuary. However, as I soon found out, tourists are fickle and you can't rely on the English weather. On wet and dreary days barely anyone came through the gates. I don't blame them really. I was out there come rain or shine because I had to be. But if I'd been on holiday, I would probably have stayed in the warm too. The problem was that the donkeys still needed caring for during the winter, regardless of whether visitors were coming or not.

Not long after moving to Huttoft, I'd given up working in the video shops. With so much to do around the sanctuary, I needed to be there full-time. Instead, I began thinking about how else I could bring some money in. That's when I decided that breeding sheep would be a good idea. After all, I had plenty of land.

So I purchased nine ewes, a male sheep also known as a tup, and a sheep rearing handbook. I resisted Steve's offers of help. This was to be my project, and I'd figure things out for myself.

Soon enough, the ewes fell pregnant and I mentally started adding up how much I'd be able to sell the offspring for. The females would be sold on for lambing, or perhaps I'd keep them myself. Unfortunately the males would be sold for meat. That's just how things worked.

When the first of the ewes went into labour, I grabbed my handbook and headed out to the field. Flicking through the pages for tips, I was carefully watching the ewe for any signs of distress. My heart was in my mouth as the first lamb was born, covered in yellow goo. The mother immediately took to it, licking it clean and encouraging it to try to stand up. I stayed to watch, mesmerised by the bonding ritual.

It was a good job I did, because within a few minutes she gave birth to a second. Healthy twins from my first birth. I felt so lucky. I wasn't prepared for what happened next, though – she had a third. I didn't know what the chances of triplets were but I was over the moon. However, my well-thumbed book warned that with three lambs one would usually be left behind or rejected by the mother. I knew to expect that there would be a weakling who'd need hand rearing.

By the next day, it was obvious which the little reject would be. Two of the lambs were feeding quite happily, but the mother kept butting the third away. It was really sad to watch.

'Don't worry, little one,' I said, bundling up the outcast in a towel. 'I'll feed you instead.'

So I took him back to the farmhouse where I made up a bottle with a special lamb formula. He suckled it greedily, no doubt starving. Then I left him to snuggle up in a cosy corner of the kitchen to warm up.

By the end of the day I didn't have the heart to cast the lamb back outside. I couldn't bear to think of him out there alone, without his mother caring for him. He'd be cold and lonely. So I wrapped him back up in the towel, and took him up to bed with me. I can't explain why I did it, it just seemed like a good idea at the time.

I set the alarm to feed him every four hours throughout the night, and told Steve not to dare make a fuss. The little lamb needed me, I couldn't just turf him out.

He might have looked cute, but the thing about sheep is that they stink. Within a few days I'd had enough of sharing my bed, so I went up to the petrol garage in the village to see if they could spare me a large cardboard box.

'What's your name?' I asked the bloke behind the counter. 'If you can find me one, I'll name my lamb after you.'

'Well, it's Ian, but you don't have to do that,' he said, handing me a sturdy box.

'Ian it is then, thanks,' I said.

The name stuck and little Ian soon became my best friend. He'd follow me around the house, like I was Mary from the nursery rhyme. Eventually he became too big, and I set him up with a new bed in a dog kennel in the garden. He didn't hold a grudge against me, but he hated Steve for it. He'd butt him angrily in the thighs, unable to understand why Steve was allowed to live in the house with me but he wasn't.

Ian became one of the family. I couldn't go anywhere without him. He even became my sheepdog. He'd follow me through the field and the other sheep would follow him. He'd jump in the car when I was taking the dogs down to the beach, and I'd walk him along the sand too. I'd overhear people saying 'that dog looks just like a sheep', and chuckle to myself. I didn't care if people thought I was a bit strange. To me, earning the respect of an animal is worth a million times more.

5

A Desperate Plea

I waddled like the Michelin Man out to the stable block for the 10 p.m. bedtime check on the donkeys. It was early January 2009, some twenty years after I'd started the sanctuary, and the frost was well and truly biting. So I'd layered up with several pairs of long johns, two jumpers and a puffy winter coat to face the icy wind blowing through the yard. I might have looked ridiculous but at least I was well insulated. I love the outdoors, but I'd take a balmy summer afternoon any day.

Bracing myself against the bone-chilling gusts, I opened the farmhouse back gate and headed across the yard to the stable blocks. I poked my head over the wooden stable doors one by one, and shone my torch inside to make sure all my residents were happy. It was part of my nightly routine.

It was rare that anything would go wrong, but I needed that peace of mind before my head hit the pillow. I wouldn't sleep for worry unless I'd seen for myself that all the donkeys were safely bedded down for the night.

We had just come through one of our worst winters yet. It had never been my favourite season. Even Christmas didn't perk me up. I hated all the festive fuss, and had been quite happy to let the celebrations pass me by. I was glad when it was all over. No more stupid music playing in the shops, no more pressure to spend a fortune. That October had been unseasonably cold and, like my mood, the weather had only got worse from there. We'd battled ice, hail and endless rainstorms. We'd even been blanketed by thick snow, which was unusual for our part of the country. The slightly warmer sea air blowing in from the Lincolnshire coast usually saves us from that.

However, once we'd got over the worry of potentially being snowed in, we enjoyed the flurries. The donkeys didn't know what to make of it. Some of the younger ones had probably never seen snow. Soon, though, they were rolling around playing in the powder. They looked ever so cute, like a scene from a Christmas card.

That evening, I was on extra high alert. Just as old people are more vulnerable to the cold, my older donkeys were at a greater risk of falling ill or suffering from arthritis. I was especially vigilant for the smallest sign of a snuffle, dreading any of them developing pneumonia. Thanks to evolution, every autumn the donkeys naturally develop a thicker winter coat that provides them with some protection against the cold, but not enough to allow me to rest easy.

As soon as the mercury in the thermometer takes a dip every single donkey is stabled overnight, and I don't even let my group of Geriatrics out into the fields during the daylight. It's not worth the risk. And that day had been one of those exceptionally chilly days.

'Are you nice and cosy down there, Noddy?' I asked, checking in on him. He blinked back sleepily before resettling himself into a comfy position.

He'd been twelve years old when he retired from Skegness beach to the original Radcliffe-on-Trent sanctuary, back in the early days before I could even have guessed that three donkeys would become more than thirty. Nearly twenty years on, he was heading towards his twilight years. He'd certainly calmed down in that time. Now, he was one of my least mischievous characters. I think he'd decided to leave the troublemaking to the next generation, while he enjoyed the comfort of his cosy stable. His legs were a bit stiffer and he didn't have the energy for bolting around the fields with his younger friends. I still loved him just as much, though.

My ethos had always been to care for the older

donkeys with just as much passion as the younger ones. Some people give up on a donkey when it gets old, writing it off as a lost cause. But with the right care a healthy donkey can actually live well into their forties. As long as they were happy, so was I.

I finished my rounds, saying goodnight to all the residents. The local TV news had forecast warmer weather for the next day so, for that night at least, I could go to bed without worrying.

The following day, I was up well before the crack of dawn. Even though there were still hours until the winter sunrise, there was always work to be done. But first, I cooked up a huge bowl of porridge to get me going for the day, and washed it down with a strong coffee. Heading out into the cold always seemed a little bit easier with a bit of warm grub inside.

The first job of the day was to check on all the donkeys in the stables, before heaping hay into the fields for breakfast. Then we let the residents out to stretch their legs for a while. Even in the winter I tried to get them out for a bit, unless the weather was unusually bitter or wet. The chickens and ducks were let loose from their pens too. Along with the donkeys, I had a menagerie of birds that had come to me one way or another. Most of them had been dumped at the gates in boxes.

I couldn't say why people left their birds for me; they didn't tend to leave a note of explanation. They just ditched their ducks and chickens there with an assumption that I'd find something to do with them. And, of course, being the softy that I am, I did. We had chicken coops built to give them a cosy bed for the night, then during the day they'd be let out to peck around in the yard and underneath the picnic benches.

The next bit was what I always called the maid's work: clearing up after the residents. Every single stable was mucked out, the water buckets were cleaned and refilled, and the hay nets were refilled too. It was back-breaking work, but there was no way I'd put my donkeys back to bed in squalor. The best thing about summer was that the donkeys stayed out in the fields twenty-four hours a day, with temporary shelters in case they fancied a bit of shade. It made life so much easier.

There was honestly no way we'd make it through the winter without the help of our volunteers. Anyone who came to us wanting to lend a hand was always welcomed with open arms, and a shovel or a paintbrush. No matter their age or abilities, we'd find something for them to do. Don, an old man in his eighties, happily spent his days creosoting our fences. He enjoyed holidays at his caravan in Mablethorpe, away from his home in Sheffield. Being widowed, I think he felt at a bit of a loose end, so one day he turned up and asked if there was anything he could do for us. I didn't want to give an old man a heart attack but he insisted, so reluctantly I handed him a rake and pointed him in the direction of the nearest field that needed a bit of a tidy. After that, he turned up every day. Soon looking after the fences was Don's project, and he became so engrossed that often he wouldn't even pop back for a sandwich. When Don said the sanctuary gave him a reason to get up in the morning I understood completely. As long as he was happy, I was happy to find him things to do. We had other volunteers who made our garden area look pretty, or ran the bric-a-brac stall on the weekends. I was so grateful to them as every little bit helped. The one mercy was that we closed to the public completely in January and February, so that was one less thing to worry about.

After a quick break for lunch we cleaned the yard, cleared out the chicken coops, and scooped up the steaming piles of poo the donkeys had kindly left scattered around the field for us.

By early afternoon, I'd left Steve and the volunteers to bring the donkeys back in for the night.

'I'm going to get on with some accounting,' I said reluctantly. 'Come and grab me if you need me.'

It wasn't my favourite part of the job, but balancing the books was vital. Our visitor donations would spike and plummet with the changing weather, so it was especially important to keep a close eye on the accounts throughout the winter.

I scrubbed the morning's dirt off my hands, before flicking on the kettle and pulling all the paperwork out from the files in the office. I spread it out over the kitchen table, and let out a huge sigh. I'm not a computer person – never have been and probably never will be. All my admin is done the old-fashioned way, with pen and paper. Sometimes I dread looking at the figures, there in black and white to remind me just how much we're struggling financially. It's a necessary task, though. After all, the equine dentist, the vet and the farrier all work so hard for us, it's only fair that they get paid promptly.

As it was the first week of January, I'd decided to have a good look at planning for the months ahead. It's always impossible to know what to expect. After all, the donkeys don't give us a four-week warning for when they're going to fall ill. If only it was that easy. However, every summer we make a huge effort to get our account at the vet's into positive figures, so come the winter we've already got a head start on paying the bills.

This winter, however, the cold weather had cost us dearly. We'd had extra medication, several emergency call-outs, and of course vet visits for the new arrivals.

We always take in a lot of donkeys over the winter because as soon they fall ill their owners cruelly decide they don't want them anymore. As a result, that January our account at the vet's was tipping dangerously into the red.

I frowned with frustration as I totted up how much we'd spent with our feed merchant too. At the very least, I budget £100 per day for hay, bedding and food during the winter. However, we'd been forced to buy a lot more haylage for the donkeys to eat, as the snow had eliminated our readily available abundance of grass. Haylage is the next best option, as it's a special grass seed mix which is cut, dried and wrapped on a farm. The donkeys munch their way through it quite happily, but unfortunately this had also eaten away at our cash reserves.

It would be several months before we would be open to the public again, so we wouldn't be getting much in the way of donations any time soon. *Perhaps we could put an appeal in the local paper*, I thought. The reporters there were usually only too happy to help us to promote our fundraisers and events, so I mentally noted to make sure I called them later. However, no one has much spare cash in January, so I knew I couldn't bank on publicity doing the trick.

When money was tight, I couldn't help but get angry about the number of occasions we had donations stolen.

Time and time again some horrible person would sneak in with the crowds of visitors, and leave with our donation pot. They weren't stealing from me, they were stealing from the donkeys. It was so heartless. They might not have made off with that much cash, but here every penny counts.

Not for the first time, that afternoon it began to dawn on me that running the donkey sanctuary had become so much more than caring for the animals. That was the part of my day that made me smile, always, without fail. However, the bigger the sanctuary had become, the more pressure there was to keep it afloat financially. Just a few months before, it had got to the stage where either we ate or the donkeys did, so Steve did something I never thought he would. He sold his beloved motorbike to put food on the table for us and the animals. It had tided us over, but we needed more money and we needed it fast. If we'd had anything else to flog, we would have done, but I didn't have any designer glad rags or antique vases stashed away. The only alternative was to shut down the sanctuary, but I spent no more than a fleeting second considering that option. I would never let that happen. Somehow, I'd find a way to put us back on track.

It certainly would have been easier if I'd put my foot down after taking in Muffin, with only Noddy and Linda to keep him company. If I'd never started a sanctuary, never started caring so much. But then again, would I really have it any other way?

As if on cue, the phone rang, interrupting my thoughts. Desperate for an escape from the dismal numbers and depressing spreadsheets, I seized the handset and answered the call.

'Is that the donkey sanctuary?' a woman on the other end asked.

'Yep, that's us,' I said, ready to launch into my speech about how we weren't open to visitors again until March with an apology if that was disappointing. After all, that was why most people phoned.

'My sister and I have found a donkey that's not in a good way, and I was wondering whether you might be able to help,' she said.

'Oh, right, what's happened?' I asked, suddenly more interested in the phone call.

'He's been abandoned and he's ever so skinny,' her Birmingham accent drawled. 'Please help. I phoned another sanctuary, but they said no. I couldn't believe it. But apparently they're stretched to the limits and can't take in another.'

Unfortunately, that was often the case. I couldn't count the number of donkeys that had come our way after being rejected by other sanctuaries. It broke my heart that policies, space or financial restraints would get in the way of the animals receiving the help they needed. That's why I was determined that would never be the case at the Radcliffe Donkey Sanctuary. My only rule was never to take in a stallion, unless the situation was absolutely desperate. Male donkeys cause so much disruption before they are castrated, as only then do they seem to calm down enough to be handled. The last thing I need is a tearaway upsetting all the other residents.

'Can he walk?' I said, already racking my brains to think who I could phone for backup, if I needed a bit of manpower for the rescue.

'I think so. He's tied up, but he's standing so I think his legs are okay,' she said.

That was good news. At least I'd be able to handle this one myself.

'Give me the address and I'll set off now. Can you keep an eye on him until I get there?' I grabbed a pen to scribble the directions on the corner of an old invoice from the farrier.

'Of course. I don't really know what I'm doing, though. Should I feed him or something?' she asked.

'No, just try to keep him warm. I'll be there as soon as I can,' I said, hanging up without wasting time to say goodbye.

I didn't even need to ask Steve before agreeing to pick up the new donkey. We had a mutual understanding that we'd always find room for another.

It was as if the call had come from the heavens, to give me a kick up the rear end. There I'd been wondering whether starting the sanctuary had been a huge mistake. I felt ashamed that I'd let the thought of closing the sanctuary enter my mind, even just for a second. But hearing about a donkey in need reminded me why I hadn't wanted an easy life. That's why I'd packed in the job at the hairdresser's, quit the jewellery shops, and seized the opportunity to leave my mum's video-shop business. I wanted to do something that made a difference, and here was yet another chance to give an animal a future.

Hearing about a mistreated donkey never fails to upset me. Years and years of doing what I do hasn't desensitised me to that. If anything, it hits me more every single time. I automatically put myself in the donkey's place and imagine what it must be like to live with no food, no warmth, and no affection.

But I also can't help but feel angry. Defenceless animals are at the total mercy of their owners. When we get a call-out, that means that a donkey has been let down.

Sometimes it's down to ignorance and stupidity on the part of their owner, not recognising that looking after a donkey is a big responsibility requiring time and money. Other times it's down to plain cruelty.

I mean, it doesn't take a genius to work out that inside an abandoned caravan isn't an ideal home for a donkey, yet that's where we rescued Persil from back in 1996. He had a terrible wound on his nose where he had smashed his head through the caravan window. He was probably trying to escape.

At first he had real anger issues and he would kick out at anyone who dared to try to get near to him. I didn't blame him. If I'd spent my life shut in a caravan, I'd probably be angry too. But thanks to lots of patience and TLC, today he's a completely different donkey. When I walk up to him in the field the first thing he does is swing his bum round towards me – not to kick me but so I can give it a rub. There's no such thing as a bad donkey, only a bad owner.

'Steve, can you hold the fort while I go and pick up another one?' I said, striding across the yard with the car keys already in my hand.

Steve was just bolting the final stable door, with all the donkeys safely in for the night.

'And there was I thinking we were in for a nice quiet evening. Of course I can. In fact, we're all sorted so I'll come with you. What's this one's story?' he asked, concerned.

'I don't really know yet, but he's been abandoned so I'd better pick him up right away. It's over near Birmingham, though, so it might be a late one if he's difficult,' I said.

'Okay, well, we'd better hit the road,' Steve said. 'I'm sure Lesley won't mind keeping an eye on things here. She can get a stable ready for him.'

Lesley was one of our longest-serving volunteers. We'd met in our new local, the Axe and Cleaver, not long after we'd moved to Huttoft. I think she must have spotted that we weren't familiar faces, and soon we'd got chatting about the donkeys. Lesley was an animal lover too. She lived completely off-grid on the edge of Huttoft in a little cottage surrounded by four acres of land – no electricity other than a generator for occasional use and no gas. I didn't know how she did it. Those desolate few months when we first moved into the farmhouse were enough for me.

Lesley was divorced and back then she kept horses for company. She's only petite at five foot tall. Coupled with her glasses and feminine, long light-brown hair she might look like a soft touch, but I quickly learned that a horse would never dare to think they'd get the better of her. She had a natural instinct when it came to the equine species. That's not to say Lesley wasn't a people person too. She was so easy to chat to, and I warmed to her immediately. We bonded over the trials and tribulations of looking after animals.

I didn't even have to ask Lesley if she fancied lending a hand around the sanctuary every now and again, as she offered immediately. Like me, if there was a chance to help an animal, she'd leap at it. Now, whenever she's not working her seasonal job as a beach-hut operator, she's over with us. I don't know how we'd manage without her, and I'm proud to call her one of my closest friends. She might have just turned sixty but she's incredibly fit for her age, and so I have complete faith that she is more than capable of looking after everything on the rare occasion I am out and about. She won't take any nonsense from my donkeys.

Steve handed me our emergency rescue box, while he went to brief Lesley. It contained a head collar and a rope, blankets, a sedative paste just in case the donkey became distressed, and an ever reliable supply of ginger biscuits.

I grabbed the box, and started the engine of our black Toyota Hilux to back it up to hook it to our horse trailer. We were still using the one kindly donated by the Co-op all those years before. My adrenaline was already kicking in, thanks to not knowing what I'd find when I arrived in Birmingham. I was nervous, but I was also excited at the chance to help another donkey. The buzz of doing that has never worn off.

Sure, the timing could have been better. As the accounts had made clear to me just half an hour earlier, we could have done without another mouth to feed. Yet, January is traditionally a time for a fresh start, and it felt good to be on my way to give this donkey a shot at his.

6

Touch and Go

On the way down towards Birmingham, Steve and I barely spoke. I was happy to leave the driving to him. I had other things on my mind.

With any donkey rescue, I always find myself running through every possible scenario in my head. There is so much that could go wrong. Until we arrive, I don't know what kind of health the donkey will be in. Neither do I know how other people will react to us swooping in to save the day.

We'd never take a donkey without the permission of whoever it belongs to, and actually most of the time it's the exasperated owner who calls us for help. But in the case of an abandoned donkey like this one was, we're always very wary. I've had to become something of an expert at dealing with aggressive and difficult donkeys, but confrontation of the human kind isn't my thing. I'm always worried that an angry man will turn up out of nowhere to accuse us of stealing his animal.

I gazed out of the window, lost in my thoughts as frosty white fields whipped by. We were well on the way by the time Steve interrupted my worries.

'What a time to abandon a donkey, just after Christmas,' he said, as we passed the outskirts of Loughborough. 'I know we've been doing this for years, but I'll never understand what goes on in some people's heads.'

'I know,' I sighed. 'People never fail to surprise me, and not in a good way.'

It was comforting to have Steve there with me. Without him, I'd have been a nervous wreck. Since that evening when he came home to tell me he'd spotted Muffin, he'd been by my side supporting me every step of the way with whatever mad plan I came up with next.

I was the driving force behind what the sanctuary had become, but Steve was just as involved, emotionally and practically, as I was. True to our wedding vows, he was always there for better and for worse. As for 'for richer and for poorer', he was still patiently waiting for us to give the first, better option a try.

'I know you're worrying, but didn't you say the lady on the phone reckoned he was reasonably healthy?' Steve reminded me.

'She seemed to think so, yeah. But then she did admit she had absolutely no clue about donkeys,' I said.

'Well, we'll find out in about three-quarters of an hour,' Steve said, heading towards the twinkling lights of the city as the early evening winter darkness started to fall around us.

We found ourselves in an out-of-town retail park. This was exactly the kind of crowded and noisy place I hated, which was why I loved the Tesco online delivery service. But, thankfully, by the time we arrived most of the shops were closing their shutters for the day. At the far end of the car park there was a supermarket, and I could see a small group of people gathered around slightly away from the main entrance.

'Park up down there,' I said to Steve, pointing out the crowd.

As he pulled the vehicle across a couple of vacant parking spaces, a woman broke from the group and came tottering across the tarmac towards us.

'You came, thank goodness for that,' she said, wobbling on her black high-heeled boots.

I recognised her Brummie drawl immediately. She'd been the one who phoned earlier that day. But I was a bit surprised. She was dressed up to the nines, with bleached blonde hair piled up on top of her head with a sparkly clip and an expensive-looking leather handbag pulled over her shoulder. I can only guess what she must have thought of me, as I jumped out of the car in a dirty old fleece, mucky shoes, and smelling of donkey dung. She didn't look like the donkey rescuing type, which goes to show that you shouldn't make assumptions about people. I had to give her credit for doing the right thing. Hundreds of people must have ignored the little donkey, with their cash burning a hole in their pockets, while she'd cared enough to call me.

'Of course we did, I told you we would,' I said, a bit bemused. 'So, where's this donkey?'

She gestured with a carefully manicured finger over to the far corner, next to a clump of overgrown bushes strewn with empty drink cans and cigarette ends.

'He was there when I found him. It wasn't me that left him there,' she added quickly.

I didn't doubt that. A pedigree chihuahua would have been more her kind of thing, not a scruffy donkey. I walked over, and squeezed past a few more shoppers who'd put their bags of tat down to gawp.

There, in the doom and gloom, I found the cutest little dark brown donkey, shivering in the cold. My heart melted as I took in the adorable tuft of mane that flopped forward over his eyes. He hung his head in an almost sheepish way. It was as if he was thinking, *Sorry about all of this fuss.*

He'd been tied to a flickering lamp post with a dirty old rope, not more than a couple of metres long. There was no sign of any food or water left for him. But I was relieved to see that the woman had been right and he was at least standing up.

'He's been there at least a day,' the woman said, interrupting my mental analysis of the situation. 'Apparently, some travellers parked up in the car park for a few days, but when they went on their way they left him behind. It's horrible, isn't it?'

'Hmm,' I said, nodding slowly in agreement.

'When my sister and I came out shopping earlier we spotted him as soon as we parked up. We'd been planning a day of retail therapy, if you know what I mean, but we couldn't leave him there,' she said. 'No one seemed to know what to do, so that's when we found your phone number online. But my sister got a bit cold and fed up. She's waiting in the car.'

'Let's make some space then,' I said, gesturing to everyone to take a few steps back.

Then slowly, I edged closer to the animal. Since capturing Muffin, I'd become used to being kicked, bitten and shoved by new rescue cases. I wasn't worried about that anymore, and I had the scars to prove it. But I didn't want to alarm the donkey by getting close too quickly.

'Hello, who are you then?' I said soothingly as I crept towards him. He didn't even raise his gaze from the ground.

Soon I was right up in front of him. He was too broken to make much of a fuss as I reached my hand out to stroke his rough white nose.

'Here, do you want a couple of these?' Steve asked, quietly coming up behind me and holding out a handful of ginger biscuits.

'I don't think we'll need them with this one. He seems to have given up hope,' I told him sadly, grabbing a ginger biscuit anyway.

'Look what I've got for you,' I said, reaching out with the biscuit on my palm.

Only then, nostrils twitching at the delicious smell, did the donkey slowly raise his head. For a moment our eyes met, and I could sense that he trusted me already. Then, as he gently snuffled the ginger snap up and crunched it down, I took a step sideways to check out his physical shape.

He was very thin. His painfully protruding ribs told me he probably hadn't had a proper feed in his life.

'Don't worry, boy, I won't give up on you,' I whispered as I ran my hands gently over his body.

That's when, under the yellow light of the street lamp, I could see that his entire coat was absolutely crawling with lice. It was almost as if his fur was alive. It appeared to be moving all on its own. The very sight of it made me feel instantly itchy. I could only imagine what the donkey must have been feeling.

'You poor creature, how could someone abandon you like this?' I muttered under my breath. Thankfully, I'd arrived in time.

Over the years, I've seen many terrible cruelty cases. Hands down, it is the worst part of running the sanctuary. I've never got used to it; it still shocks me every time. There are a couple of rescues I know I'll never be able to forget, though. It is as if they are etched in my mind to remind me why I get up every morning.

One of the worst cases I came across was Jack, who we rescued from Gainsborough back in 1996 when we were still based in Radcliffe-on-Trent. It was actually Steve who found him. He'd gone to a farm to look at a digger for sale, and instead we ended up with a donkey. Steve took one look at the tragic conditions he was living in and knew he couldn't leave him behind. Jack was only five, but already he was at death's door.

When he arrived back at the sanctuary, the first thing I noticed was his overgrown feet. They were the worst

I'd ever seen, and it was no wonder Jack couldn't walk. But we soon discovered that wasn't the only thing causing him pain. When he was a foal someone had fitted a tight head collar on him, but as he grew larger they'd never bothered to remove it. His skin had grown over it, and it was like a permanent vice around his face. He could barely open his mouth. Even if he had been given enough food to eat, I don't think he would have been able to manage it. It was a huge job for the vet to remove it, and Jack ended up with hundreds of stitches after the major surgery.

But by some miracle he survived and, twenty years on, he's still living happily at the sanctuary. He's the most lovely donkey, and you'd never see the mental scars he must have from starting his life in such a miserable way.

Another rescue I'll never forget is Lucky, so called because she really was lucky to be alive. This was back in 1994. I'd had a tip-off that there was a donkey living in the front garden of a home in Lambley, a small village about five miles north of our old place in Radcliffe-on-Trent. I'd been warned she wasn't in a good way, but even I was gobsmacked.

We picked her up covered in massive infected ulcers, where she'd rubbed herself raw in a desperate bid to get relief from a lice infestation. She couldn't walk, her belly was full of worms, her teeth were so overgrown that she couldn't eat, and to say she was already half dead doesn't do it justice. But despite that, the owner was seemingly reluctant to let her go. I don't imagine he really cared; he probably just seized the opportunity to make a bit of cash out of me. So I ended up having to fork out £50 for Lucky, before spending all weekend crying at the awful thought of possibly having to have her put down. I bet her owners wouldn't have shed a single tear, though.

Lucky was so poorly that I couldn't put her with the other donkeys. I didn't want them to catch her infections, and I also needed her close by to keep an eye on her around the clock. So she started her recovery in the back garden of our house. Steve, to his credit, didn't dare complain when I suggested bashing out the back wall of our garage so we could use it as a makeshift stable. Soon the dust had cleared and Lucky was safely enclosed in our back garden. She was far too poorly to cause a scene, so the neighbours barely even noticed she was there.

Just a week later, the TLC had started to pay off and her condition took a turn for the better. The local newspaper even ran a piece on her miraculous recovery, alongside a very cheesy photo of us both. I clipped it out and kept it in the office as a memento.

Lucky lived in our garden for three months in all. I began to rebuild her strength by taking her for a walk up and down the road, in preparation for her eventually joining the other donkeys in Island Lane. Then one afternoon I'd just turned the corner with Lucky in tow when a woman rushed out of a house and hugged me without saying a word. I was completely taken aback, as I didn't think I'd ever even seen her before.

'Thank you so much,' she said, emotion cracking her voice.

'That's okay. But what for?' I asked, totally confused.

'I swore to my husband that I could hear a donkey at night, but he was having none of it. I thought I was going mad. Now I can tell him I was right all along,' she said. 'I genuinely thought I'd been hallucinating, but it's a real donkey.'

I couldn't help but laugh. I guess we did look an unexpected sight tramping up and down the road together. Lucky lived at the sanctuary for four blissful years, until one day she lay down in an awkward way and broke her leg. When that happens there's nothing a vet can do, and I sobbed as I gave the go-ahead to have her put down. The only glimmer of positivity was that she was an old lady, and we'd given her a few years of happiness at the end of her life.

When I think about what some of our donkeys have

been through, my blood boils. In my book, there's a big difference between people who aren't equipped to take care of a donkey, and those who wilfully mistreat them. It makes me so angry to think about how cruel people can be.

Whenever I turn up at rescue situations like Lucky's and Jack's I really have to work hard to hold my tongue. I remind myself that the most important thing is to get the donkey out of there. There's no point wasting time yelling at the people who've let their animal get into that state. I doubt they'd listen anyway. It's plain to see that the donkey is in pain, and if they've chosen to turn a blind eye, there's nothing I can say that would get the message into their thick heads.

As much as I love running the sanctuary, in a perfect world there wouldn't be any need for it. But for as long as people are mistreating their donkeys, I'll be there to pick up the pieces.

Back in the supermarket car park, the next hurdle was to get the donkey into the horsebox as quickly and as easily as possible. If a donkey has spent its life getting in and out of a trailer, like a seaside donkey would, it's a lot easier to tempt them inside. They might not want to get in, but at least they don't have the fear of the unknown. However, if they've never been in a horsebox, a donkey can kick up a real fuss. I don't blame them – I wouldn't want to be shut in a dark, scary box either.

By now, lots of the bystanders had loaded up their cars and gone home. That was a relief. It's always easier to work without an inexperienced audience shouting out their not-so-helpful hints. I asked Steve to open the horse trailer's rear doors while I worked my fingers into the knot where the rope had been tied around the lamp post.

'Should I do something to help, or . . . ?' asked the woman who'd called us, glancing at the dirty donkey and then her pristine tight blue jeans.

'We've got it under control. You just stand back out of the way, please,' I said. I could swear I saw a flicker of relief in her eyes. Her posh designer jeans wouldn't be going in the bin that evening after all.

I loosened the rope, and then walked around to face the donkey again. I crouched slightly to level my head with his, so I could look directly into his deep brown eyes.

'We're going to take you to your new home now. You're going to love it. There's grass, and warmth, and you'll make lots of new friends. But you're going to need to get into my cosy horsebox first,' I said.

I'm not daft, I knew that he wouldn't understand a single word I said. But at the very least, I hoped my voice was reassuring.

The donkey just stared back at me, a lost look in his eyes.

'Come on then, let's get this done,' I said, pulling the rope ever so slightly.

I held my breath waiting to see how the donkey would react. To my instant relief, he took one tentative step towards me. This was good news as I didn't fancy plan B. The little donkey would easily have been light enough for me and Steve to pick up, one at each end, and carry him into the horsebox. But the thousands of lice didn't make that a particularly appealing option.

'Chuck us another few biscuits and I think we'll be fine,' I called over to Steve.

'Let's hope so. It's already going to be late by the time we get back,' he said, rustling the packet.

I waved the biscuits out in front of me, tugging encouragingly on the rope again. Gradually, step by step, the donkey limped forward on his overgrown, split hooves. He let me lead him right up to the horsebox ramp, then, with just a few moments of hesitation, he hobbled all the way inside. I don't think he had the strength to refuse.

I made sure he was safe and secure, ready for the drive back. Then I gave him one last ginger biscuit.

'Well done, that's the hard bit over,' I said to him. 'Now, sit tight and we'll take you to your lovely new home.'

I secured the rear breast bar to stop the donkey

slipping around inside and swung the horsebox doors closed with a gentle click. I turned just in time to see the donkey's rescuer waving him goodbye.

'Right, we'll look after him now. Thanks again for phoning us,' I said to her.

'No, thank you for coming. I don't know what I'd have done with him if you hadn't. I don't think he would have fitted in my car,' she said with a little laugh. 'He will be okay, won't he?'

'He's not in a good way, but we're used to that. Don't worry, he'll see the vet as soon as we get back to the sanctuary,' I said. 'Why don't you give us a ring in a few days, and we'll let you know how he's getting on.'

'I will, definitely. And maybe I'll come to visit him when you're open in the summer,' she said.

I just smiled, not expecting to see her again. Nearly every time we picked up an unwanted donkey the owner would promise us a generous donation in the post to say thanks. Needless to say, the cheques never arrived. But this woman didn't owe us anything; the donkey wasn't her responsibility to begin with. I was just glad she'd made the call when she did. One more night in the cold and that poor donkey might not have survived. I didn't tell her that, though; I didn't want to alarm her.

'Right, we need to go,' Steve said, jangling the keys to push the point home.

So we said goodbye, and as we pulled out of the miserable, dark car park I was glad that was the last time the little donkey would ever see it.

'I'll phone Lesley with an ETA, and I think I'll ask her to get the vet over too,' I said as we started the 130-mile journey home. 'I don't think we should risk waiting until the morning, just in case.'

I told myself that the little donkey would pull through. He had to. But there was something about him that worried me. It was as if his spirit had been completely broken. That's never a good sign. I've known donkeys to give up on life altogether, and refuse to eat or drink no matter how I try to tempt them.

'Let's hope there's no traffic. The sooner we get back the better,' I said to Steve, willing our newest resident to hang on in there. Once he saw the miles of lush countryside and met his new donkey friends, he'd have something to live for.

7

A Donkey with No Name

The return journey to Lincolnshire felt even longer than our fraught dash to Birmingham had been. We pulled over several times to check on our new donkey. I wanted to make sure he wasn't getting distressed or upset. But I needn't have worried. Just like in the car park, he couldn't muster the energy to make a fuss.

Eventually, by late evening, we pulled through our metal gates and rumbled up the stone-flecked track towards the yard. The other donkeys heard us arriving from their stables, and some of them shattered the night-time silence by braying in welcome. Lesley was there to meet us, blankets and other supplies at the ready.

'How did you get on?' she asked hopefully, as Steve and I clambered down from the horsebox cab.

'Well, we've got him,' I said. 'That was no trouble at all really. But he's not in a good way.'

I took a quick peek into our isolation stable to make

sure it was ready. We have one dedicated block where we always put the new arrivals, slightly away from the other donkeys. Lesley had already made it cosy for our newest resident.

'He's a cute one, isn't he?' Lesley said, shining a torch into the back of the horsebox. Steve had already got the doors open ready to unload.

'I know. How could anyone not want him?' I said.

So it wasn't just my heart the donkey had melted. His little face and sad eyes were irresistible. As I stepped into the trailer and made my way down the partitioned side, I could see that he still had that same sheepish expression. He reminded me of Eeyore.

'Come on then, let's get you sorted,' I said, untying his rope. 'We've got a lovely stable ready for you.'

He barely gave a flicker of interest. But, obediently, he hobbled down the ramp behind me.

'I see what you mean,' said Lesley, getting a good look at him for the first time. 'Those hooves, ouch.'

'You should be grateful it's too dark for you to see the lice. He's absolutely full of them,' I said.

'Well, it's just as well that Norrie will be here any minute now.'

Norrie Chapman had been our vet ever since we arrived in Huttoft. She'd come highly recommended by Matthew, our old vet, and she'd lived up to the lofty expectations he'd given us. She's the owner of Rase Veterinary Centre in Market Rasen, and from the first day I met her I knew we were in safe hands. She was slim, tall and well groomed, but I quickly realised she hadn't got a hint of vanity. She was ready to get stuck in and get her hands dirty. Plus, she certainly knew her stuff and the donkeys seemed to trust her too. They'd be seeing a lot of her, so if they were happy, I was happy too.

This was the umpteenth time we'd phoned Norrie for a late-night call-out, but she breezed in looking as perky as ever. I don't know what her secret was, but she was always so fresh-faced and pretty. If I was the type of woman to care about that kind of thing, I'd be incredibly jealous. Fortunately, I've long given up on looking glam.

'You've got another then?' she asked. 'How's he doing?'

'He'd been abandoned in a car park, of all places,' I explained. 'He's very thin and he's covered in lice. There doesn't seem to be anything major, but he's feeling very sorry for himself. I'm a bit worried about pneumonia, though, as I don't know how long he's been out without a shelter.'

Unlike horses and mules, donkeys aren't naturally waterproof. That's why it's so important for them to have at least a shack, if not a stable, during the winter.

If the cold and wet weather penetrates their coat, they can go downhill in just three or four days.

'I'll do a full check, don't you worry. And what are we calling you?' Norrie said, turning her attention to our little donkey.

That was a good point. Some donkeys come to us with a name already, and we'd never change it. It's said that it is bad luck to rename a donkey, and mine usually needed all the good fortune they could get. However, I had no idea what this donkey was called. That was assuming his previous owner had even bothered to give him a name.

'I haven't really thought about it yet. When you've seen as many donkeys as I have you kind of run out of ideas after a while,' I said, racking my brains.

'Well, we can't keep calling him "him". What shall I write on all the forms?' Norrie said.

We've had all sorts over the years. Teddy, Mabel, Hannah, George. I don't always go for human-sounding names either. I've got Dolly Daydream, Oklahoma Lewis, Yo Yo. With some donkeys the name comes to you once you get to know their personality. But I didn't have the luxury of that with this one. There was no time to sit down for a ponder when his life was at stake.

'How about Alan?' I said, plucking the name almost out of nowhere.

'Sounds good to me,' said Steve, popping his head around the door after clearing up the horse trailer.

Actually, as I looked at the little donkey, Alan seemed to suit him. It was a steady, sensible sort of name. That seemed to sum him up down to a tee. It wasn't the name for an extrovert or a mischief-maker, and our new donkey obviously wasn't one of those.

'Alan it is then,' I said.

I watched with admiration as Norrie gave Alan a full health MOT. She knew every little niggle to watch out for, thanks to the years of training she'd committed to. Every time I see Norrie at work I can't help but remember my early ambitions to be a vet. She knows so much, and I can't even imagine being in her shoes.

'I'd put him at just under two-and-a-half years old,' she said, trying to catch a look at his teeth.

That's the most accurate way to age a donkey. The teeth completely give it away until they reach the age of twenty, and then it becomes a bit more difficult.

'I see what you mean about the lice too,' she said, grimacing as she parted his coat. 'But, I'm sure you know how to deal with that.'

'That's the first job as soon as you're done,' I said. 'I'm not having them crawling all over the place.'

Then she reached into her medical supplies box for a couple of vials.

'You're not going to like this, but I've got some nasty jabs for you,' she said soothingly to Alan.

All of our donkeys receive tetanus and flu shots as soon as they arrive. The last thing we need is for them to come down with a new illness. Alan barely flinched as Norrie injected him with each immunisation.

'He's a good boy, isn't he?' she said.

'He's been like that since we picked him up. We'll see how he gets on with some food in a bit,' I said. 'Then I'll be able to tell what kind of mental state he is in. Maybe he's just exhausted, but he doesn't seem to have much of a spirit.'

'Well, physically speaking I don't think there's anything major going on for me to treat. There are no signs of pneumonia. Just a few more of the usual bits and pieces for me to do, then I'll let you take it from there,' she said.

And, as if right on cue, Alan dropped a steaming pile of donkey poo right next to Norrie's boot.

'Well, that's the dung sample sorted,' she said, laughing.

She scooped some up into a plastic container and sealed it. We always make sure our new donkeys have a worm count, where their poo is looked at under a microscope to check whether they need worming treatment. It's important to do the test first, because if a donkey has got a lot of worms the wrong type of treatment can actually kill them. And if they don't need worming, overusing the treatment can leave the donkey resistant to the drugs.

'I'll get back to you with the results as soon as they're ready. That's me done, but do give me a call if you need anything else. I'll be back at any time, day or night, you know that,' she said reassuringly.

I regularly thanked my lucky stars for Norrie's five-star twenty-four-hour service.

'You're in good hands here, Alan,' she said, with a little chuckle. 'Tracy will have you up and about in no time.'

I hoped she was right. I waved Norrie off, then headed over to the tack room to grab the clippers.

'Right, Alan, I can't put you to bed with all of those lice,' I said, revving the motor.

Forlorn, he raised his head to see what I was going to put him through next. I couldn't bear the thought that he was expecting me to hurt him.

'It's absolutely painless, I promise. You'll feel so much better afterwards.'

Bless him, he stood there patiently while I clipped away his entire winter coat, lice and all. It was strangely satisfying to imagine those nasty little parasites falling to the floor. Underneath his fur Alan had the scabs to prove how uncomfortable he'd been. He'd almost rubbed himself raw with all the itching and scratching. Thankfully, the sore spots would soon heal. Then I went back to the tack room to grab a pungent chemical solution to pour over Alan's freshly shaved body. That would ensure that any lice that remained wouldn't survive the night.

'All sorted. Now you can have a good night's sleep without all those horrible bugs,' I said to Alan.

He wasted no time in settling himself down in a cosy corner of the stable. I could bet that he'd be asleep even before I'd pulled my welly boots off. It was probably the first comfortable night's sleep he'd had in his life.

'Night, Alan,' I whispered, bolting the stable door closed behind me.

Back inside, Steve had been waiting for me in the living room before heading up to bed.

'I told Lesley to head off home as it looked like you had things under control,' he said. 'All sorted?'

'Yep, Alan looked ever so sweet all snuggled up. I'm still really worried about him, though,' I said.

'He looked done in. What did Norrie say?'

'Well, there's nothing seriously wrong with him. But it wouldn't be the first time a donkey decides they've simply had enough of life,' I said.

'From the state of him, I wouldn't blame him,' Steve replied. 'If he could talk, I bet he'd have some shocking stories to tell.'

'I know. Anyway, I'll see you in bed. I've been dying for a shower since I caught sight of those horrible lice,' I said, scratching at my arm.

Soon I'd stripped off and turned the water up as hot as I could bear it. I scrubbed away at my skin until it was red, determined to get rid of the creepy crawly sensations. Then I climbed into bed and set the alarm on my mobile phone to wake me again in just two hours' time.

I wasn't expecting to nod off. I wouldn't sleep easy unless Alan was okay. It wasn't that I didn't trust Norrie; I knew if there was the smallest sign of sickness she'd have spotted it right away. But Alan was in desperate need of the basics we're all guilty of taking for granted – warmth, hydration and nourishment. It was my job to make sure he had them.

It felt like I'd only been asleep for seconds when the beep of my mobile's alarm jolted me wide awake. I pulled my wellies and big winter coat on over my pyjamas, and padded down to the stable. I creaked open the stable door and watched Alan anxiously under torchlight to check he was still breathing. His sighs were slow and regular – a good sign. He'd barely nibbled at the haylage

I'd left for him earlier, but he'd gulped down a fair amount of water. I topped that up and, after watching him sleep for a few more moments, I crept back to bed.

I repeated this ritual twice more that night, with nothing to report. But despite the lack of sleep, I was still up bright and early at 5.30 a.m. Alan's stable was first on my call list.

Since I'd last looked in on him at 4.30 a.m., nothing had changed. He was still slumped in the corner. When I unbolted the stable door he didn't even glance up to see who was bothering him.

'Morning, Alan. How was your room, sir?' I joked.

But still not even a flicker of a reaction. I wasn't expecting him to roar with laughter at my poor attempts at humour, but any of the other donkeys would have been snuffling at my pockets straight away, curious to see if I'd brought them any treats. Not Alan, though.

'You poor thing,' I said under my breath as I shook up his haylage and changed his water. He needed time.

I set to work on the daily jobs list, turning the other donkeys out into the fields for a while as it was a nice, bright day. I was a bit slower than usual in ticking things off as I kept wandering over to check up on Alan.

Then mid-afternoon there was a breakthrough. Only a small one, but it gave me a glimmer of hope. I caught

Alan nibbling on his food and then, as I unlocked the stable, he turned and took a few steps towards me.

'Oh, so you are interested in us after all, are you?' I said, stroking his nose.

He raised his eyes to look up at me under the floppy tufts of fur, and rubbed his face against my hand. It was as if he was saying, *Thank you for saving me*. But he didn't need to thank me. He already had a place in my heart, and I wouldn't have changed that for the world.

The next day I decided it was time for Alan to have an appointment with our farrier. He needed those awfully overgrown hooves sorted as soon as possible if I was to get him up and about again.

A lot of people totally neglect to look after their donkeys' feet. It's just as important as it is with a horse, though, even if they're not being ridden. Left untreated and untrimmed, the hooves will grow and grow until they curl under into a painfully unnatural shape. They can split too, leaving the donkey prone to infections.

I couldn't even guess when Alan had last had his hooves looked after. They were curled under like slippers, and I knew that it would be incredibly painful for him to walk.

Our farrier, Russell Nicholls, arrived later that afternoon, and I led Alan out into the yard for his pedicure.

Some donkeys hate having their feet messed around with, but from what I'd seen from Alan so far I didn't think he'd pose a problem. He seemed woefully ready to endure whatever we put him through.

'These don't look good,' Russell said, making his initial assessment by picking up Alan's deformed feet one by one.

'I know. He was abandoned so I don't have any history for him, but he's not been very well looked after,' I said.

'Well, I'll have him feeling better in no time,' Russell said, spreading out his tools and getting down to work.

I held Alan still from the front while Russell prodded, trimmed and shaped. Alan barely flinched. I had a horrible feeling that pain was all he knew. It was normal for him.

By the time Russell was done it was like a miracle had been performed. Alan's feet didn't even resemble the mess he'd been walking around on before. I wasn't surprised – I'd seen Russell at work many a time before. He is excellent, which is exactly why we call him in, time and time again.

'Much better, hey?' he said, stepping back to admire his work.

'Definitely. If that doesn't perk him up, I don't know what will,' I said.

Then I led Alan around the yard so he could try out

his new hooves. He obediently plodded around after me. I could already tell he was stepping forward without the same hesitation he'd had before.

'Well done, Alan, another step in your recovery,' I said. 'If you'll pardon the pun.'

This time, I could have sworn I caught a hint of a grin on his face.

The farrier was soon followed by the equine dentist, who sorted out Alan's overgrown teeth. It's always a big event when our dentist, Tom Grantham, turns up with his kit, because the treatment looks so barbaric. It's not something we have done when we have visitors around if we can help it.

With a donkey, it's not as simple as telling them to open wide and say 'aah'. Tom would soon have his hand bitten off. Instead, he uses a metal gag to hold open the donkey's mouth while he reaches inside. It looks a bit like an old medieval torture device. I have to admit that the first time I saw it I was quite taken aback. But in actual fact, the donkeys don't really mind it. Tom's an absolute expert at what he does, so he's in and out of their mouths in no time. He'll take out any loose teeth, check for abscesses and infections, and file down any teeth that have become overgrown. Still, with the number of donkeys to get through, by the time he's done at the sanctuary he looks like he's run a marathon with a sack of potatoes on his back.

All my donkeys have regular appointments with Tom, once a year. I'm a strong believer that prevention is better than cure. It's expensive, but I wouldn't neglect my own teeth so why would I neglect my donkeys'? Left unchecked, a donkey could easily develop colic or quickly lose weight. It's not a risk worth taking.

However, even with his freshly preened feet and sparkling teeth, Alan still remained his glum self. A few days later I decided that he was healthy enough to mix with the other donkeys but he didn't want to know. I tried to tempt him out towards the field, wiggling a carrot as encouragement. I thought if he could see the other donkeys over the fence maybe he'd perk up and want to go and play. But he just looked at the ground.

'Come on, Alan, you'll soon make friends,' I said, offering him a nibble of the carrot.

He swung his head in the other direction and plodded back towards his stable. Whatever his previous owners had done to him, it had seriously messed him up. It was almost as if he had sunk into a deep depression and didn't know how to lift himself out of it. I didn't know what the answer was, as it wasn't something I had seen before. But I would be damned if I wasn't going to try everything in my power to help.

8

The Hooligans

'Ross, you're on poo picking, I'm afraid. Lesley, you're with me cleaning the stables. And Steve, those fences really need fixing up today,' I said, organising the team for the day.

The countdown was on. We'd be opening to the public for a new season in just a couple of weeks, and we needed to get the place looking presentable.

You'd think that having two months off to ourselves would have meant we'd be more than ready for visitors again. Our depressing bank balance certainly was. But unfortunately, at the sanctuary there never seemed to be enough hours in the day to get on top of things. So that year, like every year, we found ourselves running around like headless chickens to finish off all the odd jobs before February was out.

It all felt like a bit of a waste of time. At the end of the day, we were there to look after donkeys, not to impress the public. We're not a zoo, and we've never intended to be. I think of us as an accidental tourist attraction. But still, I knew that if we wanted people to support us we needed to make them feel welcome.

'Right you are, I know my place,' Ross joked, pulling his hoody sleeves up and heading out towards the fields. He'd been volunteering at the sanctuary since the year before, doing odd days here and there. He'd quickly built up a special bond with the donkeys, and it certainly was handy having a strong thirty-something man around the place. He might look a bit intimidating – he's a big guy always dressed in a moody black hoody and baggy jeans – but appearances can be deceptive. Underneath he's softly spoken with a heart of gold and a cracking sense of humour.

The donkeys had been turned out for the day. That is, all except for Alan. Despite looking much plumper and healthier than he had when he'd arrived at the sanctuary, he was still feeling sorry for himself. Nothing I could do would tempt him outside. He seemed to prefer cowering in the stable. For the last week or so I'd been leaving the stable door open for him during the day, hoping that curiosity would get the better of him. Every morning I'd have everything crossed that that would be the day Alan would lift himself out of his deep depression.

But despite crossed fingers and toes, and countless ginger biscuit bribes, he wasn't interested.

Occasionally he'd pop his head out for a little look around. But he didn't seem in the least bit keen to go and make friends with the other donkeys. He could see them frolicking around in the fields, and it broke my heart that he didn't want to go and join them. Instead, he'd give me that downtrodden look of his, and plod back inside to mope.

Donkeys are usually really sociable animals. I wondered whether Alan had spent too many years on his own. Like a lonely kid, perhaps he didn't know how to make friends. I'd seen distressed donkeys, scared donkeys and poorly donkeys, but I'd never come across one as depressed as Alan. Usually even the most mentally damaged donkeys perked up as soon as they realised there were other donkeys playing around in the fields. Donkeys don't like missing out. But Alan didn't seem to care if the others were having all the fun without him, and I'd never come across that before.

I was determined to crack Alan, but it had been a week and I was getting worried whether he was too much of a challenge even for me. I always made sure to give him an extra bit of fuss, along with a pep talk, whether he wanted it or not. That morning I'd warned him that he wouldn't get away with moping around forever.

'I'm going to need my stable back sooner or later, you know,' I said, my voice softening as he nuzzled at my palm.

But it was no good. Alan hung his head, as if he was resigned to having to toe the line eventually. How could I get cross at a donkey as beaten down as he was?

So, with Alan still moping, we all got on with the jobs for the day. I went to the tack room to grab the brushes for me and Lesley, and we got stuck in on the first stable. But then, suddenly, the companionable silence was shattered by an almighty bray.

Donkeys' voices are as unique as humans'. After spending so much time around my lot, I could pick out each of their brays with my eyes closed. But this was like nothing I had ever heard before. The sound was almost ear-shatteringly painful, striking a pitch that set my teeth on edge.

'What on earth was that?' I said to Lesley, clattering my broom to the floor in surprise.

'I have absolutely no idea.' She popped her head out to look around the yard.

Then she turned back to me with a grin on her face.

'You need to have a look at this, Tracy,' she said.

As I stepped out into the yard, I couldn't believe my

eyes. Alan was finally out of his stable. Even better, he'd wandered over to the gate leading into the field where some of my naughtiest donkeys were nibbling at the grass. He turned his head to look at me, before opening his mouth again. I covered my ears against the noise as he let out a roar of sound.

'Alan's finally found his voice,' I said, laughing despite the assault on my ears.

'And what a voice it is,' said Lesley with a grimace.

'Who'd have thought such a tiny donkey could make so much of a racket?'

We watched as Alan lingered over by the metal gate. For the first time he seemed interested in what the others were up to. I could swear he even looked envious as they chased each other around. One by one, the other donkeys came up to the gate to get a good look at Alan. It was a friendship-forming ritual I'd seen many times before.

At first, I always keep the new donkey safely on the right side of the fence, so that the other residents can get used to him or her. I observe carefully to judge whether they seem to be getting on. Then, only once they've grown familiar with each other, I decide whether the new donkey would be a good fit for that group.

Alan stood patiently while introductions were made, poking his nose curiously through the metal bars. Then as the donkeys trooped back across the field he turned his head towards me as if to say, *Mum, can I go and play too?* I could hardly believe it.

'I think I'll keep him in for the rest of the day, just to be sure he's ready. I don't want him to get bullied if he goes back into a sulk as soon as he's out there,' I said to Lesley. I was well aware that I sounded just like an anxious parent on the first day of primary school.

'Good idea. What a turnaround, though,' Lesley said.

She was right. Alan had been moping around for days but it looked like he'd finally agreed with me that enough was enough. He was ready to become part of the family.

Lesley and I rushed through cleaning the rest of the stables, driven by a desperate need to get away from Alan's constant noise. Now he'd finally spoken he wouldn't shut up, calling to the other donkeys to come back to keep him company.

Over a ham bap at lunch, I gave Steve the update.

'I could hear him from over in the farthest field,' he said, munching on his roll. 'Who'd have thought Alan had it in him?'

'Not me, that's for sure. I've had sleepless nights worrying about that flipping donkey, but it looks like he was attention seeking all along,' I said, laughing.

'So much for his name. A sensible, quiet and steady

sort of name, wasn't that what you said he suited?' Steve teased.

Steve was right. Maybe my little Alan wasn't such a wallflower after all. Still, it had made my day to see his personality begin to shine.

That evening Alan seemed almost a bit downcast to be put back in his stable. But I made him a promise as he bedded down for the night.

'Get a good sleep because tomorrow you can go and make friends properly,' I said, stroking the white patch on the end of his nose.

I knew I'd sleep easier that night. Alan really had turned a corner. For the first time since seeing him shivering in the corner of that car park I felt sure he'd be fine.

As my head hit the pillow I was looking forward to waking up in the morning. My to-do list was longer than ever but I couldn't wait for Alan to start the next chapter of his life. I began to drift off into a peaceful sleep. Then, suddenly, the idyllic countryside silence was shattered. It was Alan again, letting out a noisy bray just to remind me he was out there.

'Is that what we'll get every night now then?' Steve moaned, huffing as he tossed and turned to get comfortable again.

Until that morning I'd wondered whether our little

donkey was completely mute. But there was one thing I was sure of – with Alan we would be in for plenty of surprises.

The next morning, Alan barged me out of the way as soon as I unbolted his stable door. I followed as he made his way straight over towards the gate. There was no doubt about what he wanted. He was ready to go free range.

I'd already decided that night that Alan would be a good fit for my twelve-strong gang of Hooligans. They were the naughtiest donkeys in the sanctuary, and something told me that Alan had more of a spark than he'd previously let on. Call it instinct. Alan had been trickier to size up than most of the donkeys that had come through the gates, but I was beginning to realise that there was more to him than met the eye.

The Hooligans had a reputation for causing trouble, and their favourite game was to plot escapes. In fact, it was solely down to them that I'd had to upgrade from electric fencing to solid wooden barriers. Sometimes in the night the battery would run out on the fence, and with me sound asleep they'd waste no time in making a run for it. Much to my embarrassment, I'd been woken up to calls informing me that my donkeys were snacking on flower beds down in the village and napping on people's driveways. I'd have to leap out of bed and try to herd them back home.

Even the wooden fences hadn't put paid to their taste for freedom. On a number of occasions they'd made a gap between the posts and hotfooted it out of the sanctuary yet again. I never saw how they did it as their plots always took place in the dead of night, but I knew even the littlest donkeys had an almighty kick. I wouldn't have put it past them to line up against the fence and give it a boot all together on the count of three.

As well as the Hooligans, I had the Geriatrics, which were my OAP residents, and the Mismatches, which was all of the rest. When the time was right a donkey could be moved from one group to another, but it all depended on personality.

Alan had already bonded with the Hooligans over the gate the previous day. He'd chosen his tribe himself, and that's the best way. So, after warning him to be good, I opened the gate and let him join the others in the field.

Steve brought me over a coffee and together we watched Alan's introduction into the group. I knew that the Hooligans wouldn't stand for any more of his misery, not with mischief to plan. So they sussed him out, braying noisily and nudging him as if goading him to fight for the alpha male role. Alan patiently let them size him up; he wasn't interested in becoming the boss of the group. Instead, he returned their brays but didn't bite at the invitation for a scrap. Then once the formalities were over and the pecking order was established, the group got down to business doing what they do best – causing chaos. I couldn't help but smile as I watched Alan galloping across the field, chasing the others around. It was like a game of tag but with no rules.

'I think he'll be just fine,' Steve said.

'Me too. It's just as well really, we've got work to do,' I said, thinking about how much we still had to do with opening day looming frighteningly close. 'At least that's one weight off my mind.'

For the rest of the day, I let Alan enjoy his first taste of freedom. I felt proud of him. After all, that's what we rescue donkeys for. It's no life for them to be cooped up in a tiny paddock alone or, even worse, barely well enough to stand. I rescue donkeys so they can enjoy the rest of their lives. Whether that's years or just a few months, it's always worth it.

Alan had probably never played with another donkey in his life. But watching him with the rest of them, I could tell that playful instinct had never gone away. It had just taken a bit longer to coax out of him, that was all.

As I got down to work restocking our McDonkey's

catering van and brushing the cobwebs out of our public loos, the Hooligans weren't far from my mind. They never can be. If there was ever any mischief, I could be sure it was that lot who started it.

Over the years they'd plotted secret escapes, cheeky ambushes, and any ploy they could think of to get attention. I kept a close eye on them, and I couldn't help but feel that with Alan in the gang that might be even more important than ever.

By the time the first visitors pulled into the car park at 10 a.m. on a Saturday morning a few weeks later, it was as if Alan had always been part of the sanctuary. He'd fitted in with the Hooligans right away. The next test was how he'd react to the public.

Some donkeys love a bit of fuss, whereas others are more wary. Often, those that were most neglected and mistreated are more cautious of people. However, dangle a carrot over the fence and I don't know if I've ever had a donkey who'd resist.

Within half an hour the place was swarming with people. It was great to see so many familiar faces. Lots of the locals visit time and time again, and always turn up on the first open day of the year to say hello. Those that know us best come armed with gifts. We get sacks of carrots, huge parcels of ginger biscuits, and all sorts of bits and pieces for our bric-a-brac stall. I'm always grateful, as even the smallest donation takes the pressure off.

There were also some not-so-familiar faces, holidaymakers from the coast. At that time of year it was rarely beach weather, so we were often a popular day out. For me it was a case of the more the merrier. Most of the holidaymakers are a pleasure to have around. Some even come every day for the whole of their break, and recommend us to the friends they make back at their holiday park. That's fine by me, as long as they leave a donation. We're a charity for donkeys, not for cheapskates who fancy a free day of fun on us. But the one thing I can't stand is people who don't listen to the rules.

One summer, I was approached by a woman wearing a long flowing white maxi dress, high-heeled sandals and a string of gaudy beads around her neck. As soon as she caught sight of me she made a beeline towards me.

'That man over there says I can't go in with the donkeys,' she said, gesturing towards one of my volunteers.

'Well, no, we don't let people in the fields as it would upset the donkeys,' I said. It was an explanation I'd trotted out many times before.

'I don't think that's very fair, though. I only want to go in to give them a stroke,' she said.

A child might get a bit upset at not being allowed in, and that's fair enough. They're too young to know better. But she was a grown woman, and rules are rules. But I knew her type. Some people just won't be told.

'Well, you can't really. Sorry,' I said, getting frustrated.

'But I'm on holiday and I'm really good with animals,' she insisted. 'I know absolutely everything about donkeys.'

We argued backwards and forwards for several minutes, as I got increasingly annoyed that this stupid woman just wouldn't listen. Eventually, sick of the situation, I relented. If she wanted to get into the fields, then I'd give her exactly what she wanted.

'Right, fine. Follow me,' I said, leading her over to the Hooligans' field.

'Thank you,' the woman said, giving me a smug look as she tottered into the field. It was only then that I noticed she had a roll of Polo mints clasped in her palm.

One packet of Polos and thirteen donkeys, are you mad? I thought.

As I expected, she wasn't feeling smug for long. The donkeys thought she looked like a walking, talking toy. Within seconds they were all crowded around her, jostling for the Polos. They were chomped down before

I could even blink. Then Persil grabbed hold of the flowing fabric at the bottom of her dress, and Yo Yo decided it was time to join in too for a game of tug of war. Meanwhile, Pumpkin took a bite of the beads around her neck and they pinged straight off in every direction.

'Ouch, you brutes,' she said, trying to shove them away.

She looked down at the damage and, even from my vantage point by the fence, I could see she was close to tears.

'Have you had enough fun with the donkeys now?' I called out, opening the gate for her.

She looked a right state. Her sandals kept getting caught in the gaping hole in her dress, and there was a dusty dirt patch on her bum where she'd fallen onto her arse. If only I'd had a camera. Not that she would have wanted that snap for her holiday album.

'Your donkeys are horrible,' she sniffed, before storming off. Only then did I let my massive grin show. Some people really do deserve exactly what they ask for. I don't think it was my 'horrible' donkeys that were the problem.

Within a couple of hours of us opening our gates, Alan had got the hang of making the most of the situation. We sold fifty-pence buckets of chopped-up carrots for the visitors to feed to the donkeys over the fence, and Alan soon realised that he was up against stiff competition if he wanted the tasty treats. But he had more than just his good looks on his side.

As soon as a new group of people arrived, Alan would make his way straight over to the gate and kick at it noisily with his hooves. He made sure that he grabbed their attention straight away. Then with one look at his sweet little face peering through the bars, people would come straight over. He was a charmer.

By the end of the day he'd munched his way through piles of carrots and posed for countless selfies with visitors. I'd overheard so many people commenting on how cute he was, and I agreed.

He was irresistible. That's why I'd fallen for him at first sight, under the car park street lamp all those weeks before. But what I hadn't expected was that he was the complete package, with the perfect, cheeky personality too. It was no surprise that by the end of the week Lesley's pile of applications for donkey adoptions was bulging with requests for Alan. It definitely wasn't just my heart he'd won over.

Over the next few weeks I was relieved to see that the visitors kept coming. It was just what we needed to top up our funds after the difficult winter. Alan was certainly pulling his weight in keeping the visitors coming back too. He was a hit with everyone who met him, a definite crowd pleaser.

It was just as well that our bank balance was getting a bit of a boost as it wasn't long before we had three more mouths to feed. However, these new arrivals weren't donkeys, but kittens.

For a couple of days, I kept hearing a mewing sound every time I went into the tack room. It was driving me mad, and I couldn't pinpoint where it was coming from. We did have a feral cat that lived around the yard, and despite my best efforts to tame her she was having none of it. But I'd glance out of the stable and see her lazing around in the sun on top of one of my picnic benches. It wasn't her I could hear.

I was completely bemused until one day I glanced upwards and saw three little pairs of eyes glinting back down at me from a gap up near the stable's roof. That solved the mystery: the cat had had kittens up there.

'Steve, will you bring me a ladder?' I called across the yard to where he was tinkering with the car.

'Don't tell me, you need me to fix something?' he said with a sigh, hoisting the ladder into the stable.

'Not this time,' I said. 'I think we've got kittens.'

I crept up the ladder and poked my head into the gap. Sure enough, there were three tiny little black and white kittens looking back at me. I already knew their mum was nowhere to be seen, as she was busy sunbathing.

'Hello, little ones,' I said, letting them sniff at my hand.

As I looked back down the ladder, I could see Steve rolling his eyes at me.

'I'll bring you some cat food, shall I?' he said.

For the next few weeks I felt like I was constantly back up and down that ladder, trying to tempt the kittens to come down. It wasn't just because I wanted a cuddle with them. I didn't want my sanctuary to become overrun with more cats so, as soon as they were old enough, I planned to capture them to be neutered at the vet's.

Eventually I coaxed them down and they proved to be much friendlier than their mother, who had now been named Mummy Cat. They'd loiter around for scraps at lunchtime, and soon would let us stroke them too.

Then the day came for their little op. First I needed to catch them. They were only kittens but they had definitely inherited more than a hint of their mother's wild side. So, deciding to be cautious, I put on a thick pair of winter gloves to protect myself from their sharp little claws before scooping them up. I loaded them into boxes and drove them down to the vet's myself.

'We need to register them, so what are their names?' the receptionist asked, tapping away at her computer.

'Erm, well . . .' I said, hesitating.

The thing was, the cats did have names but it was embarrassing to have to say them out loud. They weren't exactly conventional. I'd sort of named them in my head and the names had stuck.

I had Cutie Cat, who was obviously the best looking of the litter. Then there was Scaredy Cat, who it had taken much longer to win over. And finally there was My Friend, so called because when I tried to tempt her with food I'd say, 'Come over here and you can be my friend.'

So, reluctantly, I mumbled the names to the receptionist.

'Pardon?' she said loudly.

I was forced to repeat myself loudly, blushing with embarrassment and instantly regretting the silly names.

'But we call them the Three Miсekateers,' I added, as if that somehow made the situation better.

'Oh right,' the receptionist said, looking at me as if I had three heads.

If she overheard some of the 'conversations' I had with the donkeys down at the sanctuary, she'd see how mad I really was.

9

Lights, Camera, Alan!

Over the next few months, Alan really made himself at home. I felt privileged to watch his transformation from a shy, downtrodden and neglected donkey. Soon he was just like any other donkey his age should be. Carefree, playful and mischievous.

Whenever I was working in his field, scooping up dung or fixing up the fences, Alan would always be the first to come over to say hello. He'd do his best to interfere with whatever I was trying to get done. He tipped over my wheelbarrows as soon as I'd loaded them with manure, and one afternoon he even made off with my hammer between his teeth. But I found it impossible to get angry with him. At school there was always a cheeky but lovable kid in the class, who the teacher let get away with murder. At the sanctuary, that was Alan.

It's hard to explain, but from the first time I saw Alan I felt that we had a special bond. It wasn't just that he was cute, although that helped. There was something about the way he looked at me. His attitude seemed almost humble.

You could give me the most awful, badly tempered, unlikeable donkey and I'd still pull out all the stops to help them. But when you sense that a donkey really is grateful, it hits you in the heart. Alan had certainly found a place in mine.

As the days got longer and the weather got warmer, Alan seemed to really blossom. I could understand why – I was more at home in the sunshine too. The longer, brighter days made even the toughest chores more tolerable.

Summer has always been a special time at the sanctuary. In years gone by it was the most important time of the year, as it marked the season for our annual open day. I only had to think of the memories and it made me smile.

The open days started back when we were still based in Radcliffe-on-Trent. I wish I could take the credit for them, but they weren't actually my idea. That honour goes to a pair of elderly spinster sisters, Jose and Pauline Miller, who lived nearby in West Bridgford.

The sanctuary was still in its infancy at the time. We'd been up and running for a couple of years, but on a much smaller scale. The sisters had read about us in the local paper and, for some reason, they decided that my donkeys would be their project.

I was down at the field in Island Lane one day when they just turned up out of the blue. They called out to me over the fence, and I plodded over to see what they wanted. That's when they explained that they wanted to help.

'We might not be up to doing the manual work, but we're good organisers. Maybe we could do some fund-raising?' one of the sisters suggested to me.

It seemed like a good idea to me. Fundraising was never my forte, but there was no denying that the sanctuary needed some extra cash. Until that point it had mostly been coming out of my own pocket, and Steve's. I had a stable on my wish list, so the older and sicker donkeys would have a proper shelter. But there was no way I'd ever be able to afford that without help.

After chatting to the sisters for a while, I warmed to them. They were animal lovers, and I think they were really excited about finding something to do with their time. They'd never met me before, so I felt really grateful that it was my donkeys they'd chosen to help.

We swapped phone numbers and agreed that the sisters would go away and have a bit of a think about how they could encourage donations. I thought maybe they'd run a little raffle or host a coffee morning. But, as I found out when the phone rang a few days later, they had much bigger plans in mind.

'We've been in touch with Dennis McCarthy at BBC Radio Nottingham, and he's going to help with a fund-raiser,' Pauline said.

'Really? Well, that would be fantastic,' I said.

'He's a friend of ours, and together we think that we could raise the two thousand pounds you need for that stable,' she said.

I was flabbergasted. Two thousand pounds really was a lot of money, especially back then. But Pauline made it sound so easy.

'We've spoken to a builders' merchant's in Nottingham too. They're going to donate some of the materials you'll need, in return for a bit of publicity. It's all coming together nicely,' she said.

All I could say was thank you. I felt choked up with emotion that people could be so kind. And the goodwill didn't stop there. In no time at all the £2,000 had been raised, and the sisters had assembled an army of volunteers to help us to build not just one but two stables ourselves.

After that, the sisters' plans only got bigger. A few months later, they'd talked me into hosting an open day on the May bank holiday weekend. They were real go-getters, not the type of people you say no to. And why would I say no? They made the whole thing sound so simple.

'We'll make all the arrangements, don't you worry about a thing,' Jose said calmly. 'Just be ready on the day, and we'll do the rest.'

To be honest, I didn't have time to worry about what they were up to. My hands were full with looking after my ever-growing herd of abandoned donkeys so I left them to it. They'd check in with me every now and again, and I'd nod my head to say yes to whatever they were planning to do. There were talks of cake stalls, children's games, tarot card readings, and Dennis McCarthy had agreed to officially open the event.

But I soon found out that he wasn't the only famous face lending a hand. Unbeknown to me, the sisters had spent hours and hours writing off to every celebrity they could think of, asking for a donation for an auction. I don't know what they said in their letters, but they must have tugged a few heartstrings because the packages came flooding in.

By the morning of the event, they'd acquired signed books from Anthony Hopkins and Paul and Linda McCartney. Sir Andrew Lloyd Webber sent T-shirts from *Cats* and *Jesus Christ Superstar*, and Stuart Pearce, who I was reliably informed was a top player for Nottingham Forest FC at the time, donated signed shin pads.

I thought the sisters were joking when they revealed the star lot of the auction, but they were true to their word. They'd been sent a lovely plush car rug from none other than the Queen Mother herself. I couldn't believe it – we even had the backing of royalty.

The day before the open day, we spent hours in the sunshine setting up all the stalls and making sure everything was ready. I had nerves in the pit of my stomach. What if no one came?

I shouldn't have worried, though. By 10.30 a.m. we were flooded with visitors and, apparently, cars were queuing for miles down the road. To say it was a success is an understatement. It was phenomenal. By the end of the day we'd raised around £7,000, which was nearly half of our running costs for the year. The Queen Mother's rug alone went for £250.

The best thing about the open day was how it brought the community together. The village had never had such a huge event and everyone loved it. The local pubs sold out of beer, and no one even minded the traffic problems as they were all at the open day too.

I think back to that day as a real turning point for the sanctuary. Until then, it had been a little venture for me and Steve. But after the open day, we found ourselves surrounded by an army of regular supporters. We didn't have to struggle on alone anymore, and it was all thanks to the sisters.

We hosted the annual open day for several years after that, always with just as much success. Our celebrity friends stayed on board too. The next year the Queen Mother donated a fantastic set of silver teaspoons, and Frank Bruno and Gary Lineker sent auction items too. We sold drawings by Reggie Kray, a signed picture of Elizabeth Taylor, ties from Richard Whiteley and Michael Caine, and a pair of gloves worn by actress Deborah Kerr in the fifties film *The King and I*. It only came to an end when we moved to Huttoft and finally had the council's permission to open all year round. I look back on the open days with much fondness.

It was the beginning of summer, a few months after Alan's arrival, when the phone rang early one morning.

'Radcliffe Donkey Sanctuary,' I answered, still chewing on my last mouthful of toast.

'Oh, hello. I'm setting up a photoshoot in your area, and I wondered whether it might be possible to borrow one of your donkeys?' said the man on the other end of the line.

'Erm, maybe, what for?' I said.

'It's a beach-themed bikini fashion shoot and a donkey

would really finish off what we had in mind,' said the voice hopefully.

'Well, I suppose so. When do you need us?' I asked. Fashion wasn't really my thing, but I couldn't think of a reason to say no.

'In a fortnight, in Sutton-on-Sea. Would that be okay? We've hired a beach hut on the promenade,' the man explained.

'Go on then, we'll see you then,' I said.

I was a bit bemused. Somehow, over breakfast, I'd managed to get myself involved in a fashion shoot. There's never a dull day at the donkey sanctuary.

So a few weeks later, I found myself preparing for our debut into the world of style and glamour. I'd roped Lesley in too. I wasn't going to head down there to meet all those fancy fashion people on my own; I needed backup.

'Which donkey is going to have the honour then, Tracy?' Lesley asked, as we dished out the donkeys' dinner the night before the shoot.

'Well, I'm not really sure what they want. The man just said a donkey. I was wondering about Alan, though?' I said hesitantly.

I'd been mulling it over ever since the man had phoned a fortnight earlier. As soon as I'd stepped outside that morning, Alan had caught my eye. He was loitering over by the fence, cocking his head confidently to one side. When he saw me he stood dead still, as if he was posing. There's no way he could have known about the phone call, but it seemed as if he was pitching for the job. His gaze was saying, *Pick me, pick me!*

After everything Alan had been through, perhaps he did deserve a chance. He'd come on so much in the months that he'd lived at the sanctuary, so it would be nice to make him feel special as a bit of a reward. And, in my amateur opinion, he certainly had the looks for the camera. Perhaps I was biased, but I thought he'd look gorgeous in the shots.

'The only question is whether you think he'll behave himself?' Lesley said, hitting the nail on the head. That was my one concern too. Was Alan a bit too cheeky?

We both turned to look at him as we chatted, and there he was standing in the yard like butter wouldn't melt in his mouth.

'Look at him. How can we not take him?' I said, laughing at his innocent expression.

So the next morning Lesley helped me to give Alan the star treatment.

First of all we gave him a good wash, paying particular attention to the dusty backs of his legs. Then that was followed by a thorough brushing. Alan's hooves were already in good nick, thanks to a few repeat visits by the farrier. So the final touch was a lashing of hoof oil to make them really gleam.

Alan loved all of the attention. I think it gave him a bit of an ego boost to have Lesley and me fussing over him so much. By the time we were done Alan looked camera ready, but the same couldn't be said for us. We were soggy and covered in hair.

'Do you think they'll want us on camera too?' Lesley joked, striking a ridiculous pose.

'I bloody hope not. I'm nominating you for that job if they do. And don't argue, I'm the boss,' I said, looking down at the state of me.

There was just enough time to tidy ourselves up before we loaded Alan into the horse trailer and set off to Sutton-on-Sea, a couple of miles down the road.

The fashion people had got special permission for us to drive right along the promenade, so I flicked the hazard lights on and we made our way down past the beach huts. I could see the photoshoot a mile off. All the equipment was sprawled over the prom and down onto the sand.

As I hopped out of the driver's seat, the man from the phone call came over to say hello immediately.

'It's so nice to meet you,' he gushed.

'We've brought Alan with us. I hope he's what you were after?' I said, leading Alan down onto the concrete.

'He's perfect, absolutely perfect,' the man drawled. 'Look at him, he's adorable.'

'So, what happens next?' I asked.

'We're just getting Katie, our model, ready then we'll get started. This is fantastic. We couldn't have a seaside photoshoot without a donkey, could we?'

It's true that seaside donkeys are a really big part of the culture in Lincolnshire. In fact, the first time I ever saw a donkey was on a family holiday at the beach near Skegness.

By the age of six or seven I'd already started horse riding classes. So when I saw kids riding donkeys up and down the beach, I immediately wanted a go. I begged my mum for my little stash of holiday pocket money, and she handed it over with a typical mumsy warning.

'When it's gone it's gone, so don't come begging for more,' she said with a shrug.

Much to my disappointment, she was right. As I counted out my coins I knew I wouldn't get many donkey rides for my dosh. So I came up with a cheeky plan.

'Can I lead your donkeys for you?' I asked the man in charge of the donkeys plodding up and down the sand.

'Hmm, what's the catch?' he asked.

'A free ride?' I suggested hopefully.

'Go on then. Take that one, she won't cause you any trouble,' he said, gesturing to one of the older, bored-looking donkeys.

Soon there was a small child aboard and I tugged at the donkey's rope to get her to start walking. I led her down to the sea, then we headed back. I didn't really need to do much, as the donkey knew the drill. I spent hours going backwards and forwards while the owner took the money and put his feet up.

Then, after a while, I'd done enough hard graft to earn my free ride. It was worth every moment.

Now I'm older and I spend all day every day surrounded by blooming donkeys, my opinion on donkey rides has changed somewhat. I'm not against them. Some donkeys even enjoy them. The problem that I have is with the welfare of the donkeys.

The guidelines say that a donkey can carry a person weighing up to eight stone. I find that shocking. That's how much some adult women weigh. Plus, they only have to be given one day off per week.

It's fine for a donkey to plod up and down the sand with a small child on its back, but carrying a hefty weight day in and day out can really take its toll. I've found that out myself, the hard way.

Linda, one of the first donkeys to join Muffin, was retired from the seaside. She'd carried so many people over the years that her spine was damaged beyond repair. It was so dipped that when it rained heavily she'd have a puddle on her back.

We did everything that we could to keep her pain free, so she could enjoy her freedom at the end of her life. But despite that, one day in the field her back simply snapped. It was sickening. There was nothing that the vet could do, and she was put to sleep. I cried and cried when we lost her. I know a donkey can't live forever, but Linda shouldn't have died like that. It was all down to being ridden on a daily basis by people who were too heavy. How is that a fair life for an animal?

So seaside donkey rides might be an important tradition, but think of the donkeys. I always tell people to get to know the owner before deciding whether to pay for a small child to have a ride.

Down at Sutton-on-Sea, the photoshoot was nearly ready to begin. It was a lovely warm and sunny day but, with all the kids at school, it was quiet down at the beach. The model, Katie, came tottering out of one of the beach huts with the make-up artist trailing behind her.

'This is Alan, he'll be in the photos with you,' said our guy, making the introduction.

Katie couldn't have appeared less impressed if she tried. She glanced down at my lovely Alan with a faint look of disgust on her face. If only she'd seen him when he'd been covered in lice, then she really would have been repulsed.

'I don't really like donkeys,' she sniffed.

'Well, just pretend that you do,' the man blustered, guiding her down to the sand and beckoning for Alan and me to follow.

Katie sighed and held out her hand to take the rope from me. But there was a problem. Alan had suddenly decided that he wasn't so up for the photoshoot either. As soon as he put his hoof down onto the sand he immediately snapped it back to the safety of the prom.

'Come on, Alan,' I hissed. 'It's only sand.'

'Is there a problem?' Katie snipped.

'No, no. He just needs to get used to the sand. I don't think he likes the texture,' I said apologetically.

Katie rolled her eyes. I felt panic rising inside me, and I looked desperately over to Lesley for help.

'Let's walk him up and down the prom, and then back down onto the sand,' she suggested. 'He'll be on the beach before he knows it.'

I kept everything crossed that she was right. I could already imagine the embarrassment of having turned up with the one donkey in the world who hates the beach. As far as I knew, Alan had never been a seaside donkey. He'd probably never even seen the shore before.

Thankfully, with the lure of a trusty old ginger biscuit, we got Alan down onto the sand. I handed him over to Katie, and then hustled back out of the view of the camera lens. Katie looked doubtfully down at Alan's tough hooves and then her own bare feet, and took a big step away from him.

'Come on, let's get started while the light is still good,' the photographer said.

Lesley and I watched from the prom as the photographer started snapping away. Katie posed and pouted in her blue polka-dot bikini.

'Show the product, darling, show the product,' the photographer directed, and Katie obediently stuck out her chest that little bit more.

Alan stood next to Katie ever so patiently, as she manoeuvred into different positions around him. His tail swished lazily in the breeze. He seemed to be enjoying his day out.

'This is great. Alan is just what we needed,' the man who'd booked us said, watching from the sidelines.

I was mesmerised. It was like a different world, and our Alan was part of it. I felt really proud of him. He wasn't the same scruffy, scrawny donkey that he'd been a few months before. He'd come a long way since then.

'Show the product,' the photographer called out again.

This time, Katie swung her hip to the side, and let her gauzy beach wrap trail out behind her.

'And hold that pose,' said the photographer, crouching down in the sand for a low shot.

Suddenly, a gust picked up Katie's wrap in the wind and it whipped in front of Alan's face. With a flick of his head, he caught it between his teeth and tugged firmly.

'No, let go right now,' Katie shrieked, tugging back.

Alan thought this was great – it was like a game. Donkeys love playing tug of war, but they usually have to make do with sticks they find in the field. But this was even better.

Then, after a firm pull, Katie staggered backwards as Alan released the wrap. The stylist dashed over and, frowning, checked it for teeth marks.

'I think it will be okay,' she said, giving me a dirty look. It wasn't my fault that Alan wanted to play.

Katie shot Alan a glare too. Then, with a tight grip on the wrap, she started posing again.

I breathed a sigh of relief. That was a lucky escape, Alan hadn't ruined the shoot.

'Thank God, they probably would have asked me to pay hundreds for the stupid bit of fabric,' I hissed to Lesley.

But just as I began to relax again, Katie let out a squeal of alarm. This time Alan was tugging at her tie-sided bikini bottoms, and he wasn't going to let go. The game with the wrap had been his warm-up.

'Get off me!' she screamed, holding on to the bikini for dear life.

I rushed over to try to help. If my donkey left her there on the beach completely starkers, I'd never be able to show my face in Sutton-on-Sea again.

'No, Alan! Look at this instead,' I yelled, waving a ginger biscuit as if my life depended on it.

Lesley wasn't far behind. She grabbed the rope and tried to tug him away. Alan's eyes locked onto my biscuit, then he looked back at the bikini.

'Choose the biscuit, please choose the biscuit,' I prayed under my breath.

He released the bikini and gulped the ginger snap down in one. My heart was in my mouth and my cheeks were burning with shame. For several awkward seconds no one said a word. Then Katie broke the ice.

'Well, that nearly gave the dog walkers a surprise,' she said, looking over at the other beachgoers wandering up and down in the sunshine.

She'd seen the funny side, thank goodness.

'Don't worry, I would have put the camera down, promise,' the photographer joked. 'Maybe we'll just get some shots of Katie on her own now.'

He'd had enough of Alan's antics, and I didn't blame

him. I was so embarrassed, and so was Lesley. We couldn't even look at each other. Instead, we hovered awkwardly until we were given the go-ahead to head off home.

'Thanks so much for that. He's very photogenic,' our booker said, waving us off.

'You're welcome,' I replied, revving the engine and pulling away down the prom before anything else could go wrong.

I knew how close Alan had come to wrecking the whole thing. If he'd pulled Katie's bikini off, it would have taken more than a ginger biscuit to tempt her back out of the beach hut.

'Well, that was fun,' said Lesley sarcastically.

Finally, out of view of the fashion team, we burst out laughing. Alan might be cute, but he was a total handful. Who'd have thought such a small donkey could cause so much trouble?

10

In Too Deep

It's a cliché, but the good old British weather really is unpredictable. It certainly keeps us on our toes. One day we're preparing for a scorching weekend packed with visitors, and the next we're rushing donkeys into the stables in the pouring rain.

Thankfully, the summer of 2009 had been a warm one on the whole. For the most part, the donkeys spent the night happily in the fields instead of being cooped up in the stables. They prefer it, and I do too. It's one less job, not having to bring them in at night then clean out the stables the next morning.

Then early one morning in July, I was woken up by a donkey's cry shattering my dreams. I sat bolt upright in bed, and picked up my mobile to check the time. Quarter past five, not long until it was time to get up. The donkey's cry came again and this time, being a bit more awake, I could tell it was Alan. I'd know that racket anywhere.

It roused Steve too.

'He must be desperate for his breakfast, greedy bugger,' he said, rolling over to catch a final fifteen-minute kip.

'Hmm,' I agreed. But at the back of my mind a little alarm bell was ringing. Sure, Alan was our noisiest donkey. And I wouldn't put it past him to get us out of bed early just because he fancied a bit of attention. He was cheeky like that. Still, though, it was very out of character for him to be causing chaos this early in the morning just for the sake of it.

So, bleary-eyed, I trudged out of bed and cracked the curtain back a few inches. To my surprise, the ground was covered with puddles. It must have rained overnight – a lot.

If we'd known, we would have brought the donkeys in. Heavy rain certainly hadn't been forecast. I religiously checked the local TV weather bulletin every single day.

As I was out of bed anyway, I decided to go down to check on the donkeys. If the fields were particularly soggy, it would be best to bring them into the stables to dry off before they got too muddy. So I quickly changed out of my PJs, pulled an old baseball cap over my hair, and headed out across the yard. Field by field, I checked on all the donkeys. First, I did a quick count to make sure they were all present and correct. Then I cast my eye over the ground to make sure it wasn't too soggy. The last thing I wanted was the donkeys getting stuck in the mud. So far, so good.

Finally, I got to the Hooligans' field.

'One, two, three, four . . .' I counted under my breath. But I was one short. Surely that couldn't be right? I counted again, and realised with horror that my first count had been correct. One of the donkeys was missing. What's more, Alan was loitering strangely down at the far end of the field. Usually he'd be straight up by the gate nuzzling at my hand for treats. In a heart-stopping moment I realised that something wasn't right.

I was just about to go into the field to investigate when Steve came out to join me.

'There was no way I was getting back to sleep after that racket,' he said. 'Everything okay?'

'I don't think so, Alan's being really strange. And one of the donkeys is missing,' I said, mentally doing a roll call in my head. 'It's Dona Pepa.'

Dona Pepa was one of our more exotic donkeys, as she'd come all the way from Spain. She was originally found by a German lady who lived out there and had a soft spot for donkeys. At twelve years old, Dona Pepa was no longer wanted by her owners for working on the farm, and she was set to be sold for salami. But the kind German lady was determined to rehome her. Somehow, after making desperate phone call after desperate phone call, she ended up in touch with me.

We'd never rescued a donkey from abroad before. But the woman's last-gasp plea made me really want to help. Typically, Spanish people don't have the same fondness for donkeys that we do here in the UK. It's a culture thing. They are commonly slaughtered for meat, so people think of them more like cows or sheep. The woman was adamant she'd never find anyone to adopt this poor donkey in Spain, and we were her only hope.

Dona Pepa was special too. She was an Andalusian donkey, which is thought to be one of the oldest European breeds. Nowadays, they are incredibly rare. We had a chance to do our bit in promoting the breed, as well as saving another donkey from a sad ending. How could I refuse?

So, after a bit of research, I ended up scraping together £900 to have Dona Pepa transported here. That was back in 2007 and she settled so well that she thought she was in heaven. Then, when Alan arrived, they became firm friends. You could say that he fell for the larger lady. Andalusian donkeys are quite big in stature, and she certainly dwarfed my sweet little Alan.

It was no wonder that Alan had been acting strangely that morning. If something had happened to Dona Pepa, he wouldn't be happy.

Steve and I dashed down to the end of the field where the cause of Alan's distress was immediately obvious. Dona Pepa had slipped down into the dyke that ran along the bottom of the field. It was usually almost dry, but after the heavy rainfall the night before it had filled up with water. She was completely stuck, with her head only just poking out above the flood.

There was a look of panic in her eyes, but she wasn't making a sound. I think she was in shock. I didn't know whether she wasn't moving because she couldn't or because she didn't know what to do.

Alan was pacing up and down next to her, making tentative steps to head down into the dyke to try to save her. It would have been a disaster. He'd have gone straight under. The only reason Dona Pepa was still alive was because she was so tall.

She could have been down there for hours. But the one thing I didn't understand was how this had happened. The dyke had always been there but the donkeys usually completely ignored it. Then I caught sight of a clump of juicy-looking reeds on the opposite bank.

Suddenly it made sense. Her greedy appetite must have got the better of her, and she'd tried to lean across for a nibble. But with all the rain the bank was slippery and she had slid straight down into the water. Still, even if it had been her own fault, that didn't make the situation any better. We needed to get her out, and fast.

My first reaction was bordering on hysteria. I didn't know what to do. My donkey was drowning before my eyes. Thank goodness I had Steve there.

'I'll go and grab a head collar. You get the rest of the donkeys out of the way,' he said confidently. 'The last thing we need is another of them joining her down there.'

Alan fixed me with a firm stare, as if he was daring me to try to force him to abandon his friend.

Steve dashed back towards the stables ahead of me, while I herded the rest of the donkeys into the next field. My hands were shaking as I unbolted the gate. Sickening worst-case scenarios kept playing through my mind. *What if we can't get Dona Pepa out in time and she drowns? What if it's too late and the damage is already done?*

With the rest of the donkeys safe, I turned to Alan.

'Let us handle this. We'll look after your friend,' I said to him, pushing him back from the water's edge. 'Please, Alan, don't make this difficult.'

I felt like he understood my desperation. Reluctantly he let me lead him into the next field to join the others. He didn't want to leave Dona Pepa, but he knew that while he was taking up my attention I couldn't look after her.

We needed help, and fast. I made a frantic call to Lesley from my mobile and asked her to come in early. There was no time to explain why. I hung up, knowing she'd understand and would rush over straight away.

Within five minutes Steve was back. He'd swapped into a pair of shorts, and I gasped as he immediately plunged down into the freezing dyke beside Dona Pepa.

'Bloody hell, it's muddy down here. I think her legs must be stuck,' he said, slipping around.

He pulled the head collar over her head, and threw the rope up for me to grab. Then he reached down into the murky water to try to encourage her to release her legs from the grip of the sticky mud.

'What do I do?' I asked desperately.

'Keep a good hold on the rope, and pull as hard as you can when I tell you to. She's not going to get back up that bank easily,' Steve said, panting as he struggled to get her legs loose.

Soon Lesley arrived too, and joined me in hefting on the rope. We tried and tried, but we couldn't get Dona Pepa free enough to even put one hoof on the bank. It had been an hour, and she was still just as perilously close to drowning.

'This isn't working, we need to try something else,' Steve said, absolutely exhausted. But he didn't leave Dona Pepa's side.

'How about the fire brigade? I'm sure they have an animal rescue unit,' Lesley said, holding her hand out for my mobile.

I had no idea whether they were the right people to call; we'd never been in that situation before. But it was worth a try. I'd have given anything a go. I gave Lesley the nod, and while she made the call I tried to soothe Dona Pepa.

'They're on their way. I'll make sure the gate's open,' Lesley said, handing me back my phone. 'Maybe we should have the vet on standby too?'

This was exactly why I couldn't run the donkey sanctuary on my own. I was crumbling under the pressure of the awful situation, but thank goodness Steve and Lesley were there to tell me what to do.

It wasn't long before a full crew of five firemen from Lincolnshire Fire and Rescue arrived in a fire engine, with our vet Norrie not far behind.

'Looks like your donkey's got herself into a bit of a pickle,' the crew manager said, assessing the situation with a reassuring calmness.

'Sorry to have to call you. We didn't know what else to do,' I said.

'Don't you worry. We deal with animal rescues all the time. We'll have her out before you know it, just leave it to us.'

It wasn't long before the whole crew was assembled with straps, winches and ropes. As soon as I saw all of their equipment I knew that calling them was the right thing to do. For the first time that morning my nerves calmed slightly.

Two of the firemen plunged into the dyke to fasten the harness around Dona Pepa's shivering body. Meanwhile, Steve had a stroke of genius. Our old digger would be perfect to winch her up. Soaking wet, he dashed back to drive it over.

'We'll need blankets and anything else you've got to keep her warm,' Norrie said, giving me a reassuring smile.

'Of course. I'll go and grab everything we've got,' I said. I could tell she knew that I needed to do something useful before I lost it completely.

Lesley came back to the house with me, and we filled hot-water bottles and grabbed bundles of towels. By the time we got back down to the dyke the crew was almost ready to hoist Dona Pepa out.

I could barely watch as the digger creaked with the

pressure of Dona Pepa's weight. My heart was in my mouth. Dona Pepa's situation was critical. The straps could snap or our rickety old digger could seize up. If this didn't work, we didn't have a backup.

Slowly, inch by inch, she was lifted clear of the dyke and gently grounded back in the field. She barely twitched a muscle, and slumped onto the ground. I rushed forwards with Lesley and we held the hot-water bottles onto her shivering body, before smothering her with towels.

'Come on, you're safe now,' I said to her, willing her to hang on. She was out of the dyke, but I knew she wasn't out of the woods yet.

Norrie gave Dona Pepa a special steroid injection, while I rubbed the towels over her to generate heat. She looked up at me and I could tell she was absolutely spent. The ordeal had completely exhausted her.

'I know, I know,' I soothed her. 'We'll have you feeling better soon, though.' In truth, I was telling myself that.

'When you're ready, we'll help to get her back on her feet,' the fire crew manager said. 'We're not going anywhere.'

Eventually, after half an hour, Dona Pepa had stopped shivering and I decided it would be best to get her back to the stables if we could. Norrie agreed so I gave the fireman the go-ahead.

'Come on then, boys, on my count. Three, two, one . . .'

he said, and they all got their hands under her and heaved.

Foot by foot, Dona Pepa lifted herself up, swaying slightly. The fire crew carried on supporting her weight until we were sure she could stand. I covered her back with a dry blanket, then took the rope to lead her across the field.

'We just need to get back to the stable, then you're done,' I said to her encouragingly.

To my relief, she took a faltering step forwards, followed by another. She was flanked by two burly firemen the whole way, supporting her weight.

I kept everything crossed that she'd make it. If she collapsed again, I didn't know what we'd do. She swayed and shivered with the effort but she bravely kept putting one foot in front of the other. We passed the field where Alan and the rest of the Hooligans were. Alan was sticking his head over the fence, whinnying gently to Dona Pepa in support.

'Don't worry, she's safe,' I said to him.

It seemed to take forever but eventually we made it.

'Well done. Now you can rest,' I said, snuggling her up in the warmth with yet more blankets.

'I think you got her out just in the nick of time,' Norrie said. 'She'll need a close eye kept on her, but I know you'll do that anyway. I'll be back tomorrow to check on her, but call me if you need anything before that.'

We closed the stable door behind us and left her to get some sleep.

The firemen were packing their equipment back into the engine, and I went over to say thank you.

'I don't know what we would have done without you, thank you doesn't seem enough,' I gushed.

'It's no problem at all. These things happen,' the crew manager said.

'So, how much do I owe you? Do you send a bill or do you need the money now?' I asked. I was hoping it wouldn't be too pricey. With the vet bill on top, Dona Pepa's adventure would cost us dearly.

He cracked a grin as if I'd just told the best joke in the world.

'Oh, it's free,' he said, realising I was serious. 'You don't owe us a penny.'

'Are you sure? You're not just saying that?' I couldn't believe that they'd gone to all that trouble and I didn't even need to pay them for it.

'Of course not, all part of the service,' he said.

'Well, in that case you'd better come in for a bacon butty. It's the least I can do to say thanks.'

At the mention of a bacon bap the other lads turned towards their boss with a hopeful look on their faces.

'Well, I suppose we could. If we get another call-out, we'll have to dash off, but in the meantime a bit of grub wouldn't hurt,' he said.

So we all dried off before tucking into a roll. I couldn't credit the fire crew enough. They were lovely guys, and without them I don't know what we would have done. Soon we were all laughing away as I told them about some of our other close scrapes. They roared at my escaping donkeys and false alarms.

'I didn't know donkeys could be so much trouble,' one of the firemen laughed.

If only they knew the half of it. Eventually, they said their goodbyes and I headed back to check on Dona Pepa again. To my relief, she was looking perkier already.

'You silly creature,' I said, chiding her gently. 'If you hadn't been so greedy, that wouldn't have happened, you know? You should have just waited for your breakfast.'

Of course she didn't have much to say for herself in return. But if she could talk, I like to think that she would have said *muchas gracias*.

It wasn't just us and the fire crew she owed a thank you to. She owed the biggest thank you of all to her friend Alan. It was only down to him getting us out of bed that we found her when we did. I never expected his noisy Eeyore bray to be so useful. But it was. He'd saved her life.

The next day Norrie gave Dona Pepa a clean bill of health and soon she was reunited with Alan. If anything, the ordeal made their bond closer than ever. He followed her around the field for weeks. She'd learned her lesson, though, and curbed her appetite. There was no way she was going near that dyke again.

I wrote the fire service a letter to say thank you again, although I could never put into words how grateful I was. To them, Dona Pepa might just have been a donkey, but to me she was my friend.

Unfortunately, Dona Pepa wasn't the only animal to have a close call that summer. Unlike most of the birds I'd found myself caring for, Geraldine the chicken hadn't actually been dumped with us. Fate brought us together in an even stranger way. I was driving back from Tesco one evening, with a boot full of shopping, when she wandered out into the middle of the road. I slammed my brakes on, stopping just in time to avoid hitting her.

'Is that a little owl?' I said out loud in disbelief, peering through the windscreen.

These two bright eyes glared back at me. That's when I realised the reality was even odder than I thought. It was a chicken. She was angry, as if she was wondering what my problem was. How dare I be driving in her road? But as I looked around, I couldn't figure out where she'd come from. It was a quiet country lane without a farm building in sight.

I couldn't just leave her there. The next passing car might not be so quick to brake. But I hadn't got a clue where to return her to. She must have escaped from somewhere but by the looks of it she'd walked miles. At a loss, I got out of the car and scooped her up in my arms.

'It appears you're coming home with me,' I said, as she clucked away in indignation at being taken away from her lovely road.

I popped her on the back seat and took her home to make friends with the rest of my feathered collection.

Geraldine soon settled in, as I was able to offer her something even better than life on the road. She fell in love, hard and fast, with my white duck Jemima. Much to Jemima's annoyance, Geraldine would traipse around after her all day every day. It made me laugh to see how firmly Geraldine's devotion wasn't reciprocated. I don't really know what she expected – a female chicken and a female duck isn't exactly a match made in heaven.

For the most part, the romance was completely harmless. But problems started to emerge when Jemima decided to take a dip. At that time we had a three-foot-deep pond, although it was later filled in. Every day, Jemima would waddle down there for a bit of a paddle, and of course Geraldine would follow. When Jemima took to the water Geraldine couldn't stand being left alone on the bank and would try to follow her in. The issue was, of course, that while ducks can swim, chickens simply can't. Their feathers get heavier and heavier as they soak up the water and eventually they sink.

Time and time again I'd pluck Geraldine from the water just before disaster struck. I must have fished her out twenty times in less than a year. I'd always give her a stern telling off, reminding her that the pond wasn't for her. But sure enough her affections for Jemima would get the better of her and she'd end up back in the water.

One day, sadly, we didn't catch her in time. I found her floating on the surface of the pond, all alone. It was a tragic show of what unrequited love can do. I was so upset that we'd lost her. She was such a big character, and it left a huge gap in our lives.

11

What Friends Are For

Some people thrive on drama. Not me, though. After Dona Pepa's traumatic rescue, I was glad to get back to a bit of normality. At the end of the day, drama at the sanctuary usually meant something was going wrong. I'd quite happily forgo sick donkeys and fundraising emergencies for the quiet life.

For the next few months, things ticked along just fine. Or, at least as fine as they can when you've got more than thirty donkeys, a couple of horses and a pick-and-mix-style flock of various birds thrown in for good measure. That's not even to mention members of the public causing me unnecessary stress.

One lunchtime I was walking through the picnic area just in time to see a mum spreading out a banquet of sandwiches, crisps, cakes and who knows what else for her and her two small children. I sighed. *Here we go again*. One of my only rules at the sanctuary is that I ask people not to bring a picnic, and this mum was tucking in right next to the sign. We sell a huge range of hot and cold food and drinks, with all the profits going to the donkeys. As we don't charge people to visit I think that's more than reasonable.

So I steeled myself for a bit of an argument and went over to ask the lady to pack up her picnic.

'But my kids are hungry, what am I supposed to do?' she moaned.

'Well, you could buy some of our homemade food, or you could always have a picnic down at the beach when you leave?' I said, trying my best to be patient.

'I don't think that's very fair,' she replied, making no moves to rewrap her stacks of sarnies. 'We'll eat quickly, and you won't even notice.'

Whether I noticed or not wasn't really the point. But I had enough on my to-do list that day, and I didn't have time for a full-on debate. So, with regret, I left her to it. It was the donkeys who would lose out in the end, but I could tell she wasn't going to listen to reason.

I told myself not to let it ruin my day. It wasn't the first time it had happened, and it wouldn't be the last. Instead, I busied myself with checking the state of the fences. Then fifteen minutes later the same woman caught my eye again. This time I wasted no time in striding straight over and giving her a piece of my mind.

I caught her red-handed feeding the Hooligans chunks of pork pie, while her kids lobbed half-eaten sandwiches over the fence too.

'Stop right now! You can't give the donkeys that rubbish,' I said, absolutely incredulous.

'It's not rubbish, it's our leftovers. I thought the donkeys would like a bit of a treat,' she said, passing another piece of pork pie to Dona Pepa.

'A treat? Pah! You'll make them ill, or even kill them,' I said, barging in front of her to block her from continuing. 'I'm not exaggerating.'

At that, she finally looked a bit taken aback. I think it had dawned on her that my nice big poster asking people not to feed the donkeys without my permission was there for a reason.

'We were going home anyway. Come on, kids,' she blushed, dragging them off towards the car park before I could really let rip.

Nothing made me angrier than when people put my donkeys at risk because of their sheer stupidity. Times like that made me doubt whether welcoming the public into the sanctuary was the right thing to do. There was no way we'd get by without public donations, but if a donkey ended up poorly or dead, I'd never forgive myself.

I kept a close eye on the Hooligans for the next couple

of days, but fortunately I'd caught the woman before her 'treats' could do any damage. However, I knew that the next time I might not be so lucky.

Even when things were on an even keel there was always work to be done. I've only had one day off in the two decades of running the sanctuary, and that was thanks to Chubby Saurus, my ten-stone giant tortoise.

I was never supposed to be rescuing a tortoise. A man from a small animal centre in Kent had called to ask if I could take in one of his donkeys. He was facing tough times financially, and he knew it would be better for his lone donkey to have a companion. Treacle Toffee had lived there since he was six months old, and had never even seen one of his own kind. Of course, I couldn't refuse.

But as I got chatting to the man over the phone, I could tell he had another favour to ask. Eventually he came out with it. Had I ever considered looking after a camel?

The answer was obviously no. I had no idea what I'd do with a camel, especially one as old and cantankerous as he admitted his was. The biggest issue was that I didn't have a Dangerous Wild Animals Licence. But, almost as a joke, I asked whether he had any tortoises that he needed to rehome. Within a couple of days I was driving back from Kent with Treacle Toffee in the horsebox and Chubby Saurus in the back of the pick-up.

At first he took over my dining room while we got a shed with a heater and sunlamps built for him. Then he made himself at home with the run of my back garden to enjoy. I soon became used to his massive appetite – he could eat for England. Whenever I was at the supermarket I'd raid the reduced section for fruit and veg going out of date. He could gobble down two huge cabbages and ten bananas in one go, with a handful of pears on the side from Lesley's tree in her garden. But it would be wrong to say he wasn't fussy. He'd eat anything, but he liked me to hand-feed him. I spent hours crouched down on the floor next to him, passing him his next juicy delicacy piece by piece.

Chubby Saurus settled in and it wasn't long before he was part of the family. I loved him to bits, but unfortunately I couldn't say the same for the donkeys. Sometimes I'd let the Geriatrics graze in my back garden to give them a bit of peace and quiet, but they always gave Chubby Saurus a wide berth. I think they were scared of him – he looked like a walking rock. Even the Hooligans seemed petrified when they caught a glimpse of him through a crack in the fence, and it takes a lot to scare them.

Chubby Saurus wasn't the first tortoise I'd ever

looked after; I'd had my lovely little Walter and Betty back when we lived in Radcliffe-on-Trent but they'd both since died of old age. However, I knew I was no expert, and I wanted to pick the brains of those who were. I'd talked about wanting to visit Twycross Zoo to learn a bit more about caring for giant tortoises.

However, when I'd mentioned this to Lesley, I hadn't really been serious. I was just daydreaming. And when it came down to it, I didn't even want a day off. I couldn't contemplate leaving the donkeys for more than a few hours. What if there was an emergency?

Unbeknown to me, Lesley launched a plan to get me away from the sanctuary. I'd honestly never spent more than an afternoon elsewhere since I'd set it up, unless I was on donkey duty picking up a rescue from some far-flung corner of the UK. And even I know that that doesn't count as a break. But Lesley had decided that I deserved a day off and she was going to make sure that it happened.

Knowing me as well as she does, Lesley expected that I'd come up with a list as long as a donkey's tail with excuses of why I couldn't go. That's why she snuck around behind my back to make it happen. The first I knew of it was the day before, when she dropped the bombshell that she was staying for a sleepover.

'I'm staying over tomorrow, by the way, Tracy,' she

said casually as we were winding down at the end of the day.

'Erm, what? Are you?' That was completely out of the ordinary.

'Yep, Steve knows. It means I can look after everything while you're off on your day out. You probably won't be back until late,' she said.

'What day out?' I asked, wondering what kind of elaborate practical joke was being pulled. I wasn't going anywhere.

'Well, you're going to the zoo. Steve's taking you. Don't you dare complain, you told me you wanted to go. I decided it was about time you had a day off,' she said, laughing at my gobsmacked expression.

Steve had turned up in the yard just in time to hear the tail end of the conversation.

'Cat's out of the bag then?' he said, joining in with Lesley's laughter.

'I can't believe you two! But seriously, no. You can't do everything yourself, I'm not going anywhere,' I said stubbornly.

'Oh no, I won't be doing it all,' Lesley explained. 'I've rounded up the troops for tomorrow. Pretty much all the volunteers will be here, and I get to be the boss for the day.'

That's when I realised that I was having a day off

whether I liked it or not. Lesley had planned absolutely everything. She was ready to shoot down whatever objection I came up with.

'I don't know what to say. I don't know whether to laugh or cry,' I said. I'd been well and truly ambushed.

'Well, if you're going to cry, get it out of the way now so you can have a good time tomorrow,' Lesley said. 'I won't be making a habit of doing all the work, so make the most of it.'

That night I hardly slept a wink. Getting up for the donkeys had been my routine day in and day out for over two decades. Breaking it felt like a recipe for disaster. I trusted Lesley completely, but still, the sanctuary was my responsibility. I couldn't walk away from it, even just for one day.

Eventually, after a night of tossing and turning, it was time to hit the road. I felt dazed as I climbed into the passenger seat of the car, next to Steve. It was like a really strange dream, bordering on a nightmare. Lesley waved us off.

'See you tonight. Don't worry about a thing,' she said.

Even she knew that wouldn't happen. Of course I'd worry. By the time we'd made it fifty miles down the road to Grantham my nerves were in pieces.

'Steve, I know you'll say no but I really want to go home,' I pleaded.

'Don't be daft. Lesley will phone if she needs anything, and we're going to have a great day out. One day off won't hurt anyone,' he said.

Barring an earthquake splitting the country in two, I knew Steve wouldn't be turning the car around for anything. So I decided I'd do my best to enjoy myself.

'Let's stop for a drink. I promise not to make a run for it,' I joked, as we passed a sign for a service station coming up in a couple of miles.

'Don't try any funny business,' Steve mocked.

Soon I was stood at the counter waiting for two hot, steaming cups of coffee. *This will settle my nerves*, I thought. I always had a couple of coffees in the morning, so perhaps a hit of caffeine would kid my brain into thinking it was just a normal day. I'd gone large for good measure.

'That's seven pounds twenty then, please,' the girl behind the till said with a smile.

'Oh, that must be someone else's order. I've just got the two coffees,' I replied, rummaging in my purse for change.

'Yep, that's seven twenty for those two.' She held out her hand for the cash.

I nearly handed the coffees straight back to her, I couldn't believe it. I know I didn't go out much, but that knocked me senseless. Was that really how much a coffee cost these days?

In shock, I managed to hand over a tenner and, mouth gaping open, I carried the drinks over to where Steve had found us a seat. So much for settling my nerves. It's just as well I didn't go out more often, I'd be bankrupt.

By the time we pulled up at Twycross Zoo, I was really regretting letting Lesley talk me into the outing. I wasn't relaxed, I wasn't having fun, and I didn't see the point. But once we'd gone through the turnstile, I felt instantly more at home. Being surrounded by animals was well within my comfort zone.

As we explored the different enclosures, I even started to enjoy myself. As expected, seeing the giant tortoises was the highlight and I ended up armed with all sorts of tips from a really friendly keeper. She looked impressed when I described how much grass Chubby Saurus had to roam. But by closing time I was more than ready to go home.

We arrived back in Huttoft late in the evening. Lesley came out to greet us.

'How was it? Did you have fun?' she said.

'It was traumatic,' I told her, only half joking. 'But how were things here? Are all the residents all right?'

It was no surprise to anyone but me that the day had

gone smoothly. All the donkeys were sleeping peacefully. Life had gone on without me there cracking the whip.

That day did teach me an important lesson. I realised it was not a bad thing to rely on other people occasionally, just for a small break. I haven't had a day off since, though, and I certainly won't be asking for one anytime soon. I know where I'd rather be.

After Dona Pepa's rescue, it was only going to be a matter of time until crisis hit once more. What I hadn't expected is that she and Alan would be at the heart of it again.

The morning of the next catastrophe had been as it usually was. All the donkeys were happily playing out in the fields, leaving that day's volunteers to help me and Steve with some of the general maintenance work. So far so good.

We'd just tucked into a well-earned lunch of fish and chips from the local takeaway, a rare treat, when I spotted something strange out of the window of our tearoom trailer. Dona Pepa was lying down in the field – nothing particularly strange there. But Alan was pacing up and down beside her, nuzzling at her neck.

'Don't touch my fish, I'm not done with it. I'll be back in a few minutes,' I warned Steve.

Usually, if Dona Pepa didn't want to play, Alan would

amuse himself for a while. His actions struck me as really odd, and I wanted to go to make sure things were all right.

As soon as I got closer, I realised things most certainly were not all right. Dona Pepa's breathing was heavy and laboured, and she didn't look well at all. Alan seemed relieved to see me, as if he knew that Dona Pepa needed help.

'You look after her, I'll be back in a minute,' I said to Alan, giving him a little stroke. I needed to get Dona Pepa back to a stable and there was no way I could do that alone. Steve would have to finish his lunch later too.

Soon a whole team of us was around Dona Pepa. I slipped a head collar on her, and we tried to encourage her to stand by herself. It wasn't that she wouldn't, she simply couldn't. That morning she had been absolutely fine. Now, she'd collapsed and I didn't understand why.

The situation was looking really bleak. We'd been trying to get her to stand for hours. Sometimes donkeys do fall desperately ill for no apparent reason. I'd seen it happen before. Unfortunately, incidents like that didn't usually have a happy ending.

I couldn't bear the thought of losing Dona Pepa. She wasn't even twenty years old, no age at all for a donkey when they can easily reach their thirties and beyond.

I crouched down beside her, and rubbed her dappled grey neck soothingly.

'You are not going to die on me,' I said firmly. 'We all love you far too much. Now come on, let's get you into a stable.'

Alan rubbed his face on her neck as if he was agreeing.

Dona Pepa looked back up at us in despair with her deep brown eyes. I knew she was trying her hardest to hold on. We didn't have long.

'We're going to have to do this the hard way. We'll lift her, and see if she can stand,' I commanded Steve and the volunteers.

Everyone got their hands underneath her and, on my count, we heaved. We managed to get her back onto her feet and, for a few seconds, she swayed as if she was about to keel over again. But, with us supporting her on each side, she managed to stay upright.

There was no time to spare. We couldn't waste what little energy Dona Pepa had left, we needed her to walk to the stable while she still could.

We crowded around her, ready to break her fall as she took faltering steps back across the field. Each step was touch and go. Alan followed close behind, as if he was keeping a close eye. Somehow we made it just in time. Dona Pepa collapsed again as soon as she was inside the stable block.

I dialled Norrie's number. If anyone could save Dona Pepa, she could.

'She's breathing, but it's like there's nothing left in her. She could barely stand. It's been so sudden, though,' I explained.

'I'll be there as soon as I can,' Norrie said.

For the next half hour, all I could do was keep everything crossed and wait.

By the time Norrie arrived, nothing had changed. Dona Pepa was still as wiped out as she had been. But at least she was somewhere sheltered.

Norrie asked question after question. Had she been eating? Were any of the other donkeys unwell? She felt every inch of her body, and used all sorts of medical instruments to carry out checks. But, at the end of a very thorough examination, the cause of Dona Pepa's sudden collapse remained a mystery.

'I'll hook her up to a drip, and she can stay here tonight. Then, if she's strong enough in the morning, bring her straight over to the surgery centre and I'll run some tests,' Norrie said. 'It's best that she stays here for the time being, though.'

Just as I did whenever any of the donkeys fell ill, I got a horrible attack of guilt. I was Dona Pepa's protector, and I couldn't help but feel that I should be able to shelter her from everything. Had I missed a sign that morning when I'd dished out the haylage for breakfast?

However, my rational mind told me that sometimes these things just happen. I knew there was nothing that I should or shouldn't have done. Dona Pepa had been absolutely fine earlier. Even Norrie was mystified.

I set my alarm for two-hour intervals throughout the night to check on her. Every time I crept through the yard I was fearing the worst. She seemed to be at death's door. It was heartbreaking to see her in such a state.

By some miracle, in the morning she was still with us. So, at the crack of dawn, Steve helped me to load her into the horsebox. She was still reluctant to stand but a bit of coaxing did the trick this time. We didn't have to scoop her up off the ground like we had done the day before. I dared to hope that this was a good sign.

I drove Dona Pepa over to Market Rasen, where Norrie was already expecting her.

'She looks a little bit brighter,' Norrie remarked, as I handed the lead rope over to her.

'Maybe a little bit. She's still not right, though,' I said. Then I took a few moments to say goodbye.

In my heart, I was hoping it wasn't goodbye for good. But after losing Muffin so unexpectedly all those years before when he'd gone to the vet's for an op, I knew that there were no guarantees.

'You're not going to die on me,' I said, repeating what I'd told her in the field the day before. But this time, I was saying it as much for my benefit. 'We'll miss you but you'll be home soon.'

Then, after one final rub of her dusty grey coat, I left Norrie to work her magic.

'I'll call you as soon as there is any news,' Norrie promised.

I fiercely blinked away the tears in my eyes before heading back to the sanctuary. I was already dreading the phone ringing, not knowing whether to expect good news or bad. It was out of my hands, and I hated it.

Back home, I could tell that Alan was already missing Dona Pepa. He didn't seem to know what to do with himself. While the other donkeys were playing, he'd lost his mischievous sparkle.

The thing with donkeys is that they can form attachments very quickly. Often, they'll pick a friend for life and the two will be inseparable. It's not a romantic thing; a perfect pairing could just as easily be two male or two female donkeys. It sounds like the ideal scenario, finding your platonic soulmate. But it's only good while it lasts.

If a donkey passes away, their mate will pine for them desperately. They won't want to make other friends, as no one can live up to their lost love. A lonely donkey can plunge into a deep depression. That's why I try to discourage my donkeys from forming such exclusive pairings. It's better for them to have a group of friends. Inevitably, my donkeys do die. But this way, their loss doesn't set the rest of them on the rocks.

Alan and Dona Pepa weren't a tight pair, but I could tell they were special to each other. That's why he'd saved her from the dyke those months before. And that's why he'd been the one to stay by her side when she'd collapsed. We all need a friend and not for the first time I was glad that Dona Pepa had Alan. I just hoped, for my sake and for his, that they'd enjoy many more years of friendship.

Later that day, the phone rang. I steeled myself to answer it. It's not often I'd wish for a nuisance sales call, but on that afternoon I'd have happily taken hundreds. No news from Norrie was good news, as far as I was concerned.

But it was Norrie on the other end. She was a straight talker, so I knew that if there was bad news she'd come right out with it.

'I'd like to keep Dona Pepa in tonight,' she said, and I breathed a sigh of relief. I knew that if there was a 'but', it wouldn't be my worst fear. That the situation was utterly hopeless.

'I'm still waiting for a few test results, but she's a bit of a medical mystery,' Norrie went on.

She'd tested Dona Pepa for absolutely everything she could think of, including weird and rare illnesses I'd never even heard of. There were no answers, although the drip seemed to be helping to some extent.

Norrie promised another update the next day. I thanked my lucky stars and kept everything crossed for more improvement overnight.

By the next morning, not much had changed. Dona Pepa was still utterly miserable.

'She won't eat, and she won't stand up without a lot of persuasion,' Norrie explained. 'I'm at a bit of a loss. We can continue looking after her, but there's no medical problem for us to treat.'

The thought of her there all alone and feeling down broke my heart. I didn't want her to think we'd given up on her. That's when I had an idea.

'Do you think a bit of company might help?' I asked.

'Tracy, you know you're welcome to pop in at any time,' Norrie said.

'No, not me. How about another donkey? Maybe a friend will perk her up a bit?' I said.

It sounded like a bit of a silly suggestion. After all,

you wouldn't send your dog to the vet's just to keep your other dog company. But donkeys are different. They thrive on companionship of their own kind. I knew the nurses at the vet centre would be taking fantastic care of Dona Pepa, but it wasn't the same as having another donkey there.

'At this stage it's worth a try,' Norrie said. 'She's not got anything contagious, so there's no reason why another donkey can't come and keep her company. You're right, maybe it will help.'

As soon as the words had come out of my mouth, I knew there was only one donkey for the job. Alan would come to Dona Pepa's rescue yet again. If he couldn't give her a reason to live, then I didn't know what else we could do.

I explained my bonkers plan to Steve and he got the horsebox ready once again. For the first time in two days I cracked a small smile, thinking about how excited Alan was going to be to see his friend again.

'You're going on an adventure,' I said as I led him out of the field, much to the confusion of the rest of the Hooligans. First Dona Pepa had gone missing, and now I was taking Alan off somewhere too.

Alan hadn't been in the horsebox since his brush with fame at Sutton-on-Sea. He'd had a splendid time, so I was sure he thought he was off somewhere equally exotic as the beach. I was worried that Market Rasen wouldn't live up to his expectations. So I explained that he had a special job to do.

'You're going to the vet's, but there's no nasty medicine for you. You need to cheer Dona Pepa up for me, and make her feel better,' I said, leading him into the horsebox. I could swear there was a bit of a spring in his step as he understood his task. He was going to be reunited with his friend.

As soon as I led Alan into Dona Pepa's temporary home, he started tugging on the lead rope in a desperate bid to get to her quicker. She stood up, ears pricked to the sound of Alan's trademark ear-shattering bray.

'That's some hello,' I said, trying to calm him down.

I felt a fuzzy glow as Dona Pepa came straight over to Alan when I released him, and the pair started to groom each other. It was normal behaviour, and it gave me hope that she would be all right.

'Alan's here to keep you company until you both come home,' I told Dona Pepa, smiling at the interaction between the two of them.

'That's the liveliest she's been in days,' Norrie said, watching alongside me.

'Let's just hope it does the trick,' I replied. Dona Pepa's mysterious illness had been unpredictable. There was no guarantee that she wouldn't go downhill again.

I said my goodbyes and left my two donkeys to their affectionate reunion. Back at the sanctuary I'd just made a cup of tea when something struck me. There was total peace and quiet, without Alan creating a racket. I never thought I'd say it, but I actually missed his noise. In a way it was comforting to have him letting us know he was there. Without him, the place seemed strangely silent. None of the other donkeys' voices rivalled his, in volume or in effect.

Alan stayed at the vet's with Dona Pepa for three days. In that time she started eating again, and she got a bit of her energy back. I waited anxiously for each day's progress report from Norrie, and was delighted to hear that her health was heading in the right direction.

Then, on the third day, she called me back out to pick them both up.

'She's missing home, so I think it's about time she went back to the sanctuary,' Norrie explained. 'She needs to take it easy, though. Keep her stabled for a few days.'

'I've been so worried. Thanks so much. You saved her,' I said. I hadn't even dared to dream about bringing Dona Pepa back home, just in case the worst had happened.

'Well, I don't know about that. I think Alan deserves

more of the credit than me,' Norrie chuckled. 'I'm still none the wiser as to what caused her to collapse in the first place. But, thanks to Alan, she's back on her feet. He wanted his playmate back.'

'I can imagine. Or she wanted to come home to get away from his noise,' I said, smiling. If I was Dona Pepa, Alan's constant braying would be enough to get me up off my deathbed and sprinting down the road.

'Well, I know we'll be glad to have a bit of peace,' Norrie said knowingly.

'Try living with that screaming Eeyore every day.' I winced as Alan opened his mouth on cue.

I might have complained, but in all honesty I was glad to have my two donkeys home. It would have broken my heart to lose Dona Pepa, and Alan too. After a few days in a cosy stable she was back to her old self again, chasing Alan around in the field.

We never found out what caused her to collapse. Still, though, we ended up with a £2,000 vet bill to show for it. Thankfully, there were a number of our supporters who were as fond of Dona Pepa as Alan and I were, and we soon had donations flooding in to help us to cover it.

Yet again, Dona Pepa's adventure had had a happy ending, and we had Alan to thank for that.

12

Cruel Intentions

I squinted in the fading daylight as I herded the chickens back into their pens for the evening.

'Is that all of you?' I said, trying to count them in.

It was only 3.30 p.m. but night was already drawing close. It was one of the biggest winter challenges we faced. There were simply fewer hours in the day to get everything done. There was no point trying to do our jobs by torchlight. We'd end up stepping in countless piles of donkey poo, and I was sure some of the residents would take full advantage of that. I could imagine the donkeys roaring with laughter at us.

There was a November chill in the air, and the donkeys were feeling it too. We were back in the routine of bringing them all into the yard for the night.

'I'll start rounding them up while you finish sorting the birds out,' Steve said.

Some of the donkeys would already be up by the

gates, waiting desperately to be let in. It wasn't because they were miserable in the fields. Far from it. These donkeys would be led by their bellies. They knew that there would be a tasty pile of haylage waiting in the stable for them to tuck into for tea. That's why they were itching to get inside. Fat Annie, one of Alan's playmates from the Hooligans, would usually be at the front of the queue, with her boyfriend, Jack, never far behind. She was bossy and bolshy but he saw something in her that the rest of the donkeys didn't, and would follow her anywhere. When I first rescued her from the slaughterhouse back in 1994 I'd named her just Annie. There wasn't anything remotely fat about her. She was so scrawny that she barely even resembled a donkey. But as the months went on, she made up for lost time, spending hours munching on the grass. She became plumper, earning her not particularly complimentary nickname.

But every evening there would be a few donkeys wanting a bit of extra playtime outside, and Alan was a classic culprit in that respect. Plus, I could always bank on one or two of the older donkeys digging their heels in just for the sake of it. So while I fox-proofed the last of the chicken pens I was thankful that Steve was giving us a head start. The sooner the donkeys were in bed, the sooner I could get inside and warm up too. It was a Friday, but there was no Friday feeling at the sanctuary. We'd be open to the public as usual in the morning.

I was just about to head down to the fields when I spotted Steve in the dusky light walking back up towards me. *Maybe he needs an extra pair of hands to give Buster a bit of persuasion*, I thought. Buster was one of our oldest residents. We'd rescued him from a slaughter-house back in 1994.

At first he was really aggressive as he wasn't used to being handled. I had scars on my leg from when he grabbed me by the arm, wrestled me to the floor, and kicked at me in frustration. I couldn't blame him, he didn't know any better. Now, years on, he was much more settled. But still, he liked to assert his authority by being awkward whenever he could. That's why if I could place a bet on Buster being last in every night, I'd be a millionaire by now.

But that evening, it wasn't Buster causing a fuss.

'Some of the gates are down in the far fields,' said Steve, looking worried. 'It's really strange.'

'Are the donkeys all there?' I asked, immediately on high alert.

'I don't know yet. You'd better come and see this, though.' Steve began walking back down into the fields as I followed him.

My blood ran cold as every possible cause ran

through my mind. None of them were good. One gate off its hinges wasn't unheard of. Those donkeys had a strong kick, and a boot at the right angle could do a lot of damage. But more than one dodgy gate was worrying. My first fear was that someone had sneaked in under our noses to steal the donkeys.

As soon as I saw what Steve had seen, I knew this was no accident. The gates were bent out of shape, as if they'd been forcefully bust open. Even my biggest donkeys couldn't have managed that. But how did we not hear anything? The situation was really odd.

My first thought was to start counting the residents. I mentally ticked off the register in my head. Why someone would kidnap one of my scruffy old donkeys I had no idea, but folk can be strange. That was the worst-case scenario. The second was that the donkeys could have escaped through the open gates. Drivers would go haring round the country roads by Huttoft, and I didn't even want to imagine what would happen if one of my donkeys was loitering in the wrong place at the wrong time.

After a second tally to be sure, I breathed a sigh of relief. All were present and correct. My next worry was whether all the donkeys were all right. Had they been injured or upset? Someone had obviously been in the fields. I didn't know why, and at that point I didn't really care why. They could have been up to all sorts of no good, but as long as all the donkeys were safe then we'd cope. Property could always be replaced and damage could be fixed.

At a first glance, they didn't seem too spooked by what had happened. As usual, they had crowded around me and Steve, nuzzling hopefully for treats. All, that is, except for Alan. He was alone at the bottom of the field, pacing up and down in front of the fence.

'You round up the rest, and I'm going to see what Alan's up to,' I said to Steve.

'Right you are. I'll check them over on the way up to the stables.'

It was only then, as I was about to turn around, that I noticed dirty smears of red around the bottom of Fat Annie's hind legs. It stopped me in my tracks.

'Hang on, that looks like blood,' I said, leaning down to get a closer look.

I grabbed the torch out of my pocket to shine a bit of light on what I'd seen. Sure enough, she had a number of long cuts running around her limbs, just above the hooves. I reached out and gently touched them, to see if she was in pain. Fat Annie kicked her leg away from me. The slashes didn't look deep, thank goodness. But they were obviously sore.

'What on earth's happened there?' Steve said.

'I don't know, but those cuts will need bathing and Fat Annie's not going to like it. I'll bet that Alan knows something about it all,' I said, glancing over to where he was still pacing repetitively. It was almost as if he was standing guard.

I left Steve to check the rest of the herd for injuries while I headed down to see what was troubling Alan.

'What's been going on then, boy?' I said, as he looked over warily as I approached. 'If only you could speak, the mystery would be solved.'

He stopped in his tracks as I got closer, and he let me walk right up to him.

'Budge out the way then, let me see,' I told him, gently nudging him away from the fence.

I gasped as I saw the mess behind him. The electric fencing had been cut through and completely ripped out. The corner of the field was a hazardous tangle of wiring. As I saw the blood stains on some of the curls of wire, it was obvious what had happened to Fat Annie. She must have got caught in the debris, and pulled herself free. Whoever had been in my fields had been on a mission to get through no matter what. But at what cost? Fat Annie was injured, and they were to blame.

Suddenly, Alan's weird pacing made sense to me. He'd seen Fat Annie get injured, and had decided that he was going to protect the rest of his donkey friends from the same fate. He made an unlikely bodyguard at just waist height. But while he'd been on patrol the rest of the donkeys had stayed away from the danger zone.

'You're a good friend, Alan,' I said, scratching his favourite place by his ears. 'We'll take care of this now. It's time for bed.'

He looked up at me as if he understood. His job was done, and now he could stand down. Ever loyal to his herd, he'd kept them safe from harm. Yet again, Alan had saved the day.

Together, we walked back up towards the stable as I puzzled over what had happened. Some horrible person – or indeed people – had come into my fields, bust open my gates, destroyed my electric wiring, and rampaged their way through. But why?

As he put the donkeys to bed for the night, Steve had been wondering the same thing.

'If they were going to nick any equipment, they were heading in completely the wrong direction. Surely they'd have come straight up to the stable blocks?' he mused.

'And if they were going to nick a donkey, why would they have crossed through so many fields to do it?' I added, bolting each of the stable doors in turn.

'It's certainly a strange one. I reckon they must have come in last night. They weren't here during the day, or we'd have noticed,' he said. 'I think we had a close call. If the donkeys had been in the fields, it could have been even worse. Except for Fat Annie, the rest of the donkeys seem all right.'

'That's thanks to Alan,' I explained. 'The bastards cut through the electric fencing too, which must be how she cut her legs. But Alan was standing guard to make sure none of the rest of them trampled into the wiring.'

'Trust Alan,' Steve said, raising a small smile. 'Let's retrace the intruders' steps and see if we can figure out what's been going on.'

So together we walked the route our unwelcome visitors had taken. They'd entered from the far corner, and then headed south-west down the side of our land in the opposite direction from the village. Even as amateur detectives, we could tell they'd been in a vehicle. There were tyre marks in patches of mud along the way. And that explained why the gates had been so battered. They'd driven straight through them at full pelt.

We must have snoozed right through the racket. I could only assume that months of sleeping next door to noisy Alan had trained me not to wake up for anything. I didn't know what I would have done if I had woken up anyway. I would have panicked and got Steve up to do something, I supposed.

As we got to the end of our land, we looked up and realised what it had all been about. A scrapyard owned by one of our neighbours backed on to our furthest field. The tracks of the vandals were heading straight for it.

'They must have been trying to nick scrap metal, and we were unfortunately in the way,' Steve said.

The thought that someone had been on my land made me feel physically sick. It dawned on me just how vulnerable we, and the donkeys, were to people up to no good. We didn't deserve what had happened, but bad things don't just happen to bad people.

It turned out the scrap man had been none the wiser to the break-in either. But once we'd explained what had happened, he got straight on the phone to the police. He was really sorry that we'd been in the way, but it wasn't his place to apologise. The only people that should be sorry were the ones who'd selfishly caused the damage.

There was no use being bitter, though. That wouldn't help with the repair bill. It cost us nearly £3,000 to fix up all the damage, not to mention the time it took us too. Hours and hours of manual labour could have been hours and hours we spent making life better for the donkeys. I doubted that the vandals had even considered the knock-on effect of their actions. And even if they did, I was almost certain that they wouldn't care.

Instead, we struggled on as we always did. The volunteers rallied to get the fields secured again as soon as possible, and in the meantime I asked the *Lincolnshire Echo* to run yet another funding appeal for us. The extra cost was the last thing we needed just before heading into winter. I didn't know how we'd cope if we were faced with a repeat of the previous year's financial woes. A familiar feeling of dread gripped me as I worried about making ends meet. But I firmly told myself to save the stress for another day. There was no point worrying about things that hadn't happened yet, otherwise I'd never sleep a wink.

A few weeks later, with Fat Annie fully healed and the damage all fixed up, I had a chance to reflect on what had happened. That was, thankfully, the only break-in we'd ever had and it had shaken me. I felt repulsed, angry and scared by it. Maybe this time we hadn't been the real target, but next time we might not be so lucky.

I couldn't feel sorry for myself for long. There was always something going on at the sanctuary to make me smile. That could be donkeys being daft, generous donations from kind-hearted visitors, or just having that sense of making a difference. However, on this occasion, it was none of those. I had a new romance on the cards.

It had come out of the blue; I certainly wasn't

expecting it. My wooer wasn't even my usual type. Steve barely even noticed, and whenever he did walk in on the flirtation he'd laugh. He had nothing to worry about, though, as my new love was Jemima the duck.

After Geraldine the suicidal chicken met her tragic end, I think Jemima had been pining. She always made out that she didn't care much for Geraldine, and that the burning attraction had been a one-way thing. We'd previously had some other ducks at the sanctuary, and they'd been her gang. But they'd died and without Geraldine trailing around after her all day Jemima seemed to be a bit lonely.

I had a lovely flock of birds she could have had her pick of. The Cheeky Girls, my pair of Transylvanian Naked Neck chickens, would definitely have indulged her. After being dumped at the sanctuary by an idiot who didn't realise that they'd scratch up her garden, they quickly worked out how to maximise their charms. Visitors loved their funny antics and they were only too happy to play up to this. They'd jump on the tables and dance around, distracting people while they pinched food right out of their hands. Customers who bought chips and cake were easy prey for them. Just like their namesakes, the Cheeky Girls loved the attention. They might not have been the best-looking birds in the world – with their bare red necks they were often mistaken for turkeys. But still, they had a certain naughty-but-nice charm to them.

However, even with better options on the table, for some reason Jemima decided it was me that she fancied. Or, to be more accurate, it was my dirty green welly boots.

One morning when I let the birds out to roam, Jemima came straight over and lay down on the ground before me. Then she started to rub and ruffle her feathers over my boots, swinging her neck around and making a distinct honking noise.

I knew immediately what she was up to. I'd seen birds do it before, although never at the feet of a human. It was a mating ritual. To my disbelief, she was trying her best to attract me as a partner.

'Get away, you silly bird! I'm not going to mate with you,' I laughed, pushing her away before I tripped over

She wouldn't take no for an answer. She took every opportunity to ambush me with her best flirty behaviour. I had no idea why she'd decided my wellies and I were a match made in heaven for her. It was never going to work out between us.

But still, Jemima was nothing if not persistent. She'd even try it on with me when we had visitors at the sanctuary. It was really embarrassing having to explain to curious children what she was up to.

Her antics did cheer me up, though. It's always flattering to feel wanted, even if it is a case of unrequited love from a soppy white duck.

13

Christmas? Bah, Humbug!

'Steve, come and get a look at this,' I called through to the kitchen, from my cosy seat in the living room.

He popped his head around the door to catch what I was watching on telly.

'And from tomorrow we're expecting temperatures to plummet. So far we've enjoyed a fairly mild winter, but that will be changing from around four a.m. Expect chilly gusts blowing in from the west, with a severe risk of ice on the roads,' the BBC local weather forecaster warned.

I looked at Steve. We both knew what ice on the roads meant – ice on the fields too. The weather was turning, and not in our favour.

'Looks like we're in for a busy week then,' I said.

So far November had been surprisingly smooth, weatherwise. Other than the odd rain shower, the weather had stayed early autumn-like.

But as December got closer, I was sure I was one of

the only people around who wasn't hoping for a cold snap. Winter weather always spelled trouble at the donkey sanctuary.

I was sick of hearing visitors speculating hopefully whether it would snow for Christmas, and wondering when it would be chilly enough for snuggly hats, scarves and gloves.

I hate winter, and I hate Christmas too. If it wasn't for the donkeys, I'd be tempted to jump on any plane heading south and come back after it is all over.

Firstly, I can't stand the fuss and hysteria. At Christmas people shop like the world is ending or we are about to be hit by a national famine. When the shelves in Tesco are empty and customers are practically brawling over the last turkey, it is time to take a good look at our priorities. It's greed, pure and simple. Surely that is not what Christmas is about.

Secondly, I don't have enough time in my day for silly decorations and daft songs. Would a bit of tinsel and a poxy Christmas tree really make me feel festive? I don't think so. I'd never put up a tree before and that year wouldn't be any different.

And finally, running the donkey sanctuary is a 365-day operation. If anything, we're busier than ever at Christmas. Nothing gets in the way of that, even cele-brating Christmas Day.

One year we even got a call-out for a donkey rescue on New Year's Day. That was when we lived in Radcliffe-on-Trent. Steve and I aren't really party people, so choosing between a night packed into a busy pub or putting our feet up at home with a bottle of wine is a no-brainer. The quieter option wins every time.

Of course, one bottle turned into two and we were snoring in front of the TV long before the clock struck midnight. But in the morning there was no time to mope about with a hangover. We still had to get down to Island Lane to feed the donkeys. We were just about to drag ourselves out of the door when the phone rang.

'Sorry to call so early, especially on New Year's Day,' the male voice on the other end said.

I managed to grunt some kind of a reply.

'One of my neighbours has got this donkey, and I don't think he's looking after her properly,' he said. 'I haven't stopped worrying about her. Do you think you could do something?'

'Where is she?'

'Derbyshire. The shed's by the side of a country road, but I can give you decent directions. Please. It's been going on for months and I don't know what else to do.'

That was an hour's drive – the last thing I needed with a pounding head. But how could I feel sorry for myself when that poor donkey was in a real state? I'd get over my hangover.

'OK, we'll go and get her today,' I agreed. How could I refuse?

Steve looked just about ready to murder me when I told him that we had a job to do. I knew he wouldn't leave me in the lurch, though. Like me, he wouldn't have been able to turn a blind eye to a donkey in need.

So together we started the new year in the way we meant to go on – rescuing donkeys. When we pulled up next to the shed later that morning I was glad we had done too. The wooden shack was completely battered and the side panels were falling down. It was no home for a donkey.

I braced myself for what we'd find inside and creaked open the shabby wooden door. As I looked into the darkness, the first thing that hit me was the stench. It was like a sewer. I held my jumper up over my nose and took a tentative step inside. My foot squelched into the source of the revolting smell. There were inches and inches of old manure.

My eyes got used to the dim light and I could make out the shape of a small female donkey cowering in the corner. Her little legs were sinking into the dirt, and she was almost up to her belly in manure.

'You poor thing,' I sighed. Judging by the amount of

donkey dung flooding the ground, it had been weeks since she'd seen daylight.

Steve had opened up the trailer ready, and then he came to join me in the shed.

'Phwoar, what a state,' he said, reeling backwards from the pong.

'How could you leave a donkey in here? Why on earth would someone do that?' I asked, absolutely incredulous.

'I have no idea, but let's not have a chat about that now. Let's get her out of here before that smell knocks us out.'

Together we trudged up the lane towards the house the neighbour had told us the owner lived in. I was dying to get the donkey to safety but I had to do the formalities first. I couldn't just take someone's animal without their permission.

We knocked on the door, and thankfully the man was in. I took a deep breath to calm my nerves and my temper, and explained as briefly as possible why I wanted to take his donkey. I didn't even need to give him the spiel about our excellent facilities and the care we'd provide – he couldn't have cared less. As soon as he grunted his permission I tugged Steve away from the door and dashed back to the donkey. I had been dying to give the man a piece of my mind, but I knew better than to bother. The most important thing was to get the donkey out of there. If he'd been difficult, I wouldn't have hesitated to phone the police or the RSPCA for backup, but he seemed glad that the animal wouldn't be his problem anymore.

Back in the shack I edged towards her inch by inch. She was petrified. Her nostrils flared with fear every time I took a step closer, and her breath heaved quickly in her chest.

'Come on, I'm not going to hurt you,' I whispered in a silly sing-song voice, showing her the head collar so that there were no surprises.

The only good thing about the mountain of manure was that it rooted her to the spot. She couldn't have kicked out at me if she'd tried. I cornered her and, gently but swiftly, put on the head collar. The fear in her eyes nearly broke my heart. I knew that back at the sanctuary I'd have a lot of work to do to get her to trust me. But first I needed to get her out of the shed.

I led the way with the rope, tightening it so that she'd get the message that she had to follow. Steve held the door wide open so that she could see she wasn't being trapped. Still shaking, she trudged through the manure behind me and I led her right up into the trailer. She didn't put up a fuss, and that was purely down to shock. Her poor body didn't know what to do.

When we returned to the sanctuary, we began nursing her back to health. We treated her for a nasty lice infestation and spent hours restoring her confidence. She'd been so frightened that she'd developed stringhalt, a nervous condition that causes donkeys to snatch up their back legs as they walk. She got a name too, Holly. It was my one attempt at something festive that year. After all, it was the Christmas season.

Just like Alan had, Holly began the year with a fresh start and soon thrived. It wasn't long before she was barely recognisable as the terrified, starving donkey she'd been when we rescued her. In fact, the only sign of what she'd been through was her appetite. Like Fat Annie, she always ate as if it was her last meal, much to the disgust of the other donkeys.

I could easily have said no to the rescue, and crawled back into bed with a packet of painkillers instead. But seeing Holly's transformation started my new year in the best way possible. Donkeys like Holly are why I'm dedicated to the sanctuary every single day of the year, no matter what the occasion. If I hadn't have been there for her, who else would have been?

Despite my moans and groans, there was one part of the build-up to Christmas that I did enjoy. That was choosing my favourite photos for the sanctuary's new calendar and the Christmas cards. We sold both to raise extra funds to get us through the winter. I loved looking back through all the snaps on the computer, reminiscing about the year gone by.

Thankfully, despite the wind whipping across the fields, the sanctuary survived the previous night in one piece. So the next morning we fastened the donkeys into their warm winter coats, which had been donated by a kind supporter for when their naturally thick fur wasn't enough. Then we sent them out as usual for a bit of fresh air and exercise. I hurried through the mucking-out duties so I could grab half an hour of peace before I was needed for the end-of-the-day routine.

Eventually, I was perched in front of the computer in the office with a steaming mug of coffee beside me. It was time to get the calendar sorted. I clicked to open up my folder of pictures, and immediately felt a sense of happiness wash over me. I would challenge anyone to be stressed or depressed when flicking through albums of my cute donkeys. They never fail to make me smile.

There were shots of donkeys sprawled out in the sunshine, and frolicking in the fields. Some of them had the real 'aww' factor. The snaps of Alan were the ones that really made me grin, though. His transformation since he'd arrived had been incredible.

In the first photos, he was barely recognisable. He was loitering at the back of the field while the other donkeys hogged the limelight. He was shy, sad and scrawny. But as the year went on, you could see his confidence growing. One photo in particular really made me laugh. One morning I'd popped my baseball cap on poor Alan's head and, to my amusement, it almost suited him. He peered up at the camera from under the brim of the white hat, as if he knew just how cute he looked. That was a dead cert for the calendar. I gathered together a collection of my twelve favourites from the year, with Alan's snap number one on the list.

Then it was time to turn my attention to Christmas cards. I picked out a few featuring the Geriatrics, my golden oldie donkeys. They were well loved by lots of our visitors, so I was sure that would help to shift a few boxes of cards. But there was another I couldn't resist. I'd taken a candid snap of Alan and Dona Pepa one afternoon, grooming each other in the field. They made a comical duo, as Dona Pepa towered over little Alan. But their friendship was so adorable, and that photo really captured their special bond. That was definitely worthy of a Christmas card.

I attached all the files to an email, and sent it off to

the printer's in Loughborough. I couldn't wait to see the results. My little Alan would look fantastic in print.

Within a few weeks I'd become the postman's least favourite person. But not because of the stacks of cards I was sending out. Mine were still in their boxes, piled up ready to be written. I hadn't got round to posting a single one, and I knew by the time I did, the last postage date would be long gone. But the cards were certainly flowing in the other direction. Every day the postman would drop off a huge pile. And for every single one I got from friends and family, there were at least five addressed to the donkeys.

I couldn't get annoyed, though. It was no secret that I preferred donkeys to people, so it wasn't a surprise that people felt more fondly towards my residents than they did towards me. Plus, it always made me smile when people popped a sneaky bank note in the envelope too.

'This is so you can buy my favourite a nice Christmas treat,' they'd write, addressing their card to their chosen donkey. It was quite sweet.

A fiver here and there soon added up. It didn't really surprise me that my little Alan's treat fund was bulging more than the others. In less than a year at the sanctuary he'd captured the hearts of hundreds of visitors.

If they wanted to send us a little something to make sure he had a good Christmas, I wasn't going to stop them.

If my own house looked like Christmas had never been anywhere near it, the sanctuary's tearoom trailer was the complete opposite. I put all the donkeys' cards up so that the visitors could see how loved they were. Soon every spare inch was filled, and still the post kept flooding in.

Other than acting as the donkeys' personal secretary, for the most part I completely ignored the rest of the build-up to Christmas. Then one evening my phone beeped with a text from an old school friend.

I'm Christmas shopping this weekend – what smellies would you like? What is your favourite perfume? she asked. I snorted with laughter. Perfume, me? Surely after more than thirty years she knew me better than that.

Don't be daft! I'm after a new wheelbarrow, though, I typed.

Yeah, good joke, but seriously what do you want? she replied.

I was being serious! I answered her.

Eventually, she accepted defeat. The only pressies on my wish list were donkey related, but it never stopped people trying to tempt me. I didn't have anyone to impress with posh perfume or expensive face creams. It's not like the donkeys would care about my ever-multiplying wrinkles.

A new wheelbarrow would be great for collecting the dung from the fields and dishing out the hay. My old one had a bit of a wonky wheel. Failing that, extra head collars were always useful. My donkeys had a bad habit of destroying them.

Or, if a wheelbarrow is too much, I could always use some extra supplies of vet wrap, I texted again, having second thoughts on the wheelbarrow. I use the vet wrap to treat the horses when they have foot abscesses, so I like to keep a fair few rolls in stock.

Even Steve knew better than to try to get me a present. I certainly didn't buy him any gifts. But one year he made an exception. I'll never forget how he led me out into the yard on Christmas morning.

'I know we don't do presents, but I've got a surprise for you,' he said, beckoning for me to follow.

I was completely confused. Had he found me another donkey? Otherwise, why would my gift be outside?

But as we walked out of the garden gate into the sanctuary, all suddenly became clear. Standing in front of me was the one thing I never dared to dream of asking for for Christmas. It was a big, shiny dumper truck.

'Steve, you didn't?' I said, my eyes gleaming like most women's would when presented with a diamond.

'Well, you're always going on about wanting one, and I figured one Christmas present every once in a while wouldn't hurt,' he said, smiling at my reaction.

'It's perfect. The best present ever,' I said, wandering forward in a daze to get a better look.

It wasn't new and it wasn't fancy, but it was just what I wanted. Every day when I was breaking my back mucking out the stables by hand, heaving hay with a shovel, I'd fantasised about this moment. A dumper truck would save me so much time and effort, but there was no such thing as spare money at the donkey sanctuary. Every penny went on the essentials. But now my dreams had come true and I couldn't think of anything better.

'Thank you so much,' I said, feeling almost emotional.

Steve had kept the dumper truck hidden with a mate, ready to surprise me with it. It was one of the most thoughtful things that anyone had ever done for me. Maybe it wasn't soppy or romantic, but that wasn't my style.

December was well underway when Lesley and some of the other volunteers ambushed me over mince pies one lunchtime.

'We've been talking, and we've had an idea,' Lesley said, scanning my face for a reaction.

'Oh right, what's that then?' I replied through a mouthful of crumbly pastry.

'Well, as it's nearly Christmas we thought it might be nice to do something,' she said.

'And what kind of something did you have in mind?' I wasn't sure I liked the direction this conversation was heading in.

'Maybe something like a little party?' Lesley suggested hopefully.

'For us, you mean? Not for the donkeys?' I said. I nearly choked on my mince pie in horror. My brain was already screaming a loud and firm 'no'.

'Well, us and the donkeys really. And maybe a few other people. Perhaps some of the people from the village, and others who like to support the sanctuary,' Lesley suggested.

'I don't know, Lesley. That doesn't really sound like my kind of thing,' I said. And that was putting it mildly. No Christmas tree, no presents, no fuss was my kind of thing. Not throwing a blooming massive Christmas party. I couldn't think of anything worse.

'Oh, go on. We'll help you to organise it,' she said, pushing her luck.

'Will you now?' My mind was already made up, though.

As if it wasn't enough having the place swarming with visitors every weekend, Lesley was asking me to combine that with the one thing I hated more: Christmas. 'I don't think so. Now, come on, these donkeys won't look after themselves.'

But for the rest of the afternoon, I had a nagging feeling of guilt deep in the pit of my tummy. Lesley and the rest of them had looked so excited by their idea, and I'd given it a big fat no. On the other hand, it was my sanctuary and if I didn't want a Christmas party, why should I have one?

I was happy to forget the whole thing had ever been suggested, but it turned out that the volunteers weren't going to give up on me so easily.

'The yard would be the perfect location, and it would be no hassle to do a Christmas barbecue,' Lesley said, passing me as I wheeled through a barrow of hay.

'And the donkeys would love it,' Ross threw in.

Even Steve was tempted by the plan.

'It wouldn't be much trouble. Plus, I bet we'd get lots of donations on the night. People are always feeling charitable at Christmas,' he said, as we bolted the stables later that afternoon.

'Not you as well. I thought you were on my side with this. Since when were you Mr Christmas?' I whined. The whole thing was beginning to feel very unfair. I was being ganged up on.

'Well, it would only be a one-off. We could try it?' he said persuasively.

'I'll think about it. And that's the final word on it for now.' I hoped that maybe everyone would forget about it.

But of course they didn't. A few days later the begging and pleading started again. In the end there was only one easy option. I'd have to give in just to shut everyone up.

At least the attention would all be on the donkeys, I supposed. Everyone loves a donkey at Christmas, after all. And if on the night I had a sudden headache and needed to give it a miss, then the party would have to go on without me. Wouldn't that be a shame?

The one thing I didn't begrudge was the donkeys enjoying Christmas. In fact, a couple of Christmases before, I'd even sent one of them off to star in a local nativity play. But this wasn't any old school nativity in a poky little hall. This one was quite a big deal.

It had been organised by the community in Beesby, which was a couple of villages away. I think it was some kind of fundraiser. I only got involved because they needed a donkey. A couple of phone calls and I found myself promising to send one of my residents along. It was a bit like Alan's beach photoshoot in that respect.

For this event I chose Teddy, one of my older donkeys. He'd be perfect as, in his old age, he was far too lazy to cause any chaos. He certainly looked the part too. He was one of the sweetest donkeys I'd ever had.

So for three nights that December, Teddy got the star treatment. He was bathed, groomed, trimmed and pampered so that he looked stage-ready. Then each evening at 5 p.m. I loaded him up into the horse trailer and took him off to Beesby.

The whole village was closed off to traffic on the performance nights. People were arriving from the neighbouring villages by the coachload. I had special permission to drive right up to the barn where the nativity was being performed.

When I saw the grand setting I felt a bit nervous for Teddy. There were rows and rows of seating laid out ready. This was certainly no school play. Then Teddy was introduced to that night's Mary and Joseph.

'So, I thought maybe they'd walk in alongside the donkey? Do you think he'd do that?' the play's director asked me, clutching the script.

'He's a good boy, he'll do whatever you need him to,' I said. 'Just as long as you don't want me to get involved too.' There was no way they were getting me in the nativity as well. I wasn't walking up there in front of all of those people.

'No, no. You just relax. The children can take the rope. It won't be completely authentic as Mary can't climb aboard, but there was no way the insurance would cover that,' he laughed.

That sounded good to me. I could slip out of the beam of the stage lights and leave it all to Teddy.

By 6.30 p.m. the barn was packed, and the crowd hushed ready for the performance to begin. I hovered near the back, anxiously waiting for Teddy to make his appearance. Then Mary and Joseph set off on their journey from Nazareth to Bethlehem.

The audience cooed as the little Mary and Joseph came in from the back of the barn, walking through where the chairs were parted, followed by Teddy. Cameras flashed as he plodded loyally behind them. He was perfect for the part. Once they reached the front, attention turned to what the wise men and the shepherds were up to. I couldn't take my eyes off Teddy, though, willing him to wait patiently alongside until the baby Jesus had been born.

As the performance came to a close I breathed a sigh of relief. Teddy had been as good as gold, and the audience had loved him. The director came on to say thank you to the crowd, and they even gave Teddy a round of applause of his own. If donkeys could smile, his grin would have been a mile wide.

Soon Teddy was handed back to me. But before I could load him up to take him home, I was ambushed by the director.

'Do you mind hanging around for a little while? Some of the kids would love a photo with your donkey,' he said. 'We've got mince pies and mulled wine too.'

I couldn't really refuse. Soon Teddy was mobbed by children stroking at his face and pulling at his tail. It was a good job he was patient. The mums and dads whipped out their cameras to get snaps of their child with him, and I seized the opportunity to spread the word about the donkey sanctuary.

'We're just down in Huttoft. Come and visit when we're open again after Christmas,' I trotted out to as many parents as I could.

Eventually, every child satisfied, we were clear to head home. I'm sure Teddy slept soundly that night, exhausted by his newfound fame. He needed his beauty sleep. The show was on for the next two nights as well.

Both of the following performances went just as smoothly. I think Teddy enjoyed himself, and even I had a bit of a warm, fuzzy festive feeling by the third time I heard the kids angelically belt out 'Away in a Manger'.

So as I resigned myself to planning the sanctuary's first ever Christmas party, I clung on to the nativity memories to remind myself that perhaps Christmas wasn't all bad. If it made people smile, I'd have to grin and bear it.

14

Reindeer Games

Burgers, tick. Baps, tick. Mulled wine, double tick.

After all, you can't have a party without booze. I was checking off the to-do list for the Christmas party. Making sure we were well supplied with mulled wine was particularly high on my priority list. A glass or two might be the only thing to get me into the party spirit.

Since Lesley had bullied me into hosting the party a few weeks earlier, I had come to think the idea of a party wasn't so terrible after all. I couldn't say I was looking forward to it. That would definitely be a step too far. But seeing how excited everyone else felt was infectious. Every lunchtime, we'd chat over sandwiches and cups of tea about the upcoming event. I let myself get carried along with everyone's enthusiasm.

The party idea had started as just a little get-together for us and our closest friends and supporters. We'd put on a barbecue so people could have a bite to eat, and maybe a couple of mince pies. It wasn't going to be a big deal.

But day by day I found myself being overruled on an extra expense here, a final festive flourish there. Before I had time to put the brakes on, the guest list had swollen to several hundred. I was feeling the pressure. I hadn't even wanted to have a party, and now I was being expected to turn the place into a miniature winter wonderland.

'The things I do for these donkeys,' I sighed, adding extra sausages to my shopping list.

Then my worries were interrupted by the postman's arrival.

'Here you go, another sackload for you,' he said, rolling his eyes sarcastically as he handed over a fat wodge of envelopes.

'Thanks,' I replied sheepishly. The cards still hadn't stopped coming.

I put my shopping list to one side, and turned my attention to the post instead. The top card on the stack was in a sparkly red envelope, addressed to 'The Donkeys at the Radcliffe Donkey Sanctuary'.

'Don't worry, I'll be your secretary again,' I muttered sarcastically, catching sight of Alan and Dona Pepa out of the tearoom window.

I tore open the envelope, and shrugged at the silly

cartoon reindeer on the front of the card. As I opened it up, a fiver dropped into my lap.

Dear donkeys, I had a bit of a win on the bingo last week so I wanted to send you a little something for a Christmas treat. Merry Christmas. Love, Edna x, the card read.

I couldn't resist. A little smile twitched at the side of my mouth. I could bet that poor old Edna could have done with that fiver herself. After all, even I knew that pensions didn't pay much. But instead, she'd thought of my donkeys.

The next card on the stack was obviously from a kid. The address was squiggled across the envelope in a childlike scrawl. I pulled out the card to find myself swallowed up by a cloud of glitter. I knew it would be stuck to my trousers for the rest of the day. Great.

The card was a homemade effort, with the entire contents of someone's craft box stuck to the front. Felt holly leaves, glitter glue stars, pom poms in the corner – no expense had been spared. In the middle was what I guessed was a donkey, drawn in blue felt pen with purple legs.

Despite myself, I laughed at the image of my donkeys actually looking like that. And even I had to admit that the effort the child had gone to was touching.

Inside, they'd wished the donkeys a very happy

Christmas, and it had been signed by 'Jack aged 8'. But there was an extra message at the bottom too.

P.S. This is my pocket money for the donkeys.

I peered back into the bottom of the big brown envelope, and sure enough there were some coins jangling around. I tipped them out into my palm – £4.67, in random denominations. I guessed that Jack had spent a little bit of his pocket money first. But instead of saving the rest, he wanted my donkeys to have it.

A fuzzy festive feeling started spreading through my veins. I couldn't help it. The next card only made this worse.

It was written by a mum who'd come to visit the sanctuary with her kids in the school holidays.

I promised my daughter I'd pass on a message. She adopted Alan when we came to visit you, and the certificate has got pride of place on her bedroom wall right by her pillow. She wanted me to tell you that her Christmas wish is that more donkeys are rescued like Alan was, because she loves him so much, she'd written.

That nearly tipped me over the edge. I felt quite choked up. I knew the kids liked to come and stroke the donkeys, feeding them carrots through the fence. But it never really registered just how much of an impression the donkeys made. Trust Alan to tug on the old heartstrings, though. He really was the poster boy for donkey rescues.

Reading those cards made me stop and think. Christmas was a time for giving thanks, and all those people had bothered to pop a card in the post to acknowledge the part the donkeys had played in their year gone by. The donkeys gave them happy memories, and people wanted to give something back. It wasn't about the money that people were sending. It was, as people say, the thought that counted.

On a day-to-day basis, I found it easy to get bogged down with rude visitors and a never-ending list of things to do. I honestly believed that people visited the sanctuary because it was free, not because they were particularly interested in what we do. It was something to keep the kids quiet for an afternoon. Then, after tearing around the place causing havoc, they'd go home and leave us a snooty review on TripAdvisor about the fact we don't have a kids' play area. Well, of course we don't, we're a donkey sanctuary. We spend our money on the donkeys.

But as the cards kept flooding in, I started to feel appreciated. Sure, most of the cards were for the donkeys, not for me. Still, the fact that people had taken the time to write at all made me feel humbled.

A couple of days later, it was one week until the day of the dreaded party. So much for everyone promising to help out with the organising. I felt like I'd been running around like a headless chicken. I'd ordered in mountains of food and drink, drawn up a precise rota to get the sanctuary looking tip-top in time, and spent hours stressing myself out by worrying about whether people would enjoy themselves. Plus, in the meantime, all the usual daily jobs had to get done.

Mucking out the stables was the first thing that needed to be sorted. So I joined that day's band of willing volunteers to get stuck in. Much to everyone else's amusement, one of the girls had turned up wearing a festive headband with big fuzzy antlers attached at the top. I rolled my eyes. It would be a miracle if that was still in one piece by the end of the day.

I sent her over to grab a water bucket standing next to the gate that led into the field where the donkeys were, while I grabbed the brooms from the tack room. Then I heard a yelp of surprise.

'Give that back,' she squealed. I turned around in time to see her tugging her daft headband back from the jaws of one of my donkeys. Surprise surprise, it was Alan who was the culprit.

He'd seen the antlers wobbling around on her head as she bent down, and decided that she obviously wanted to play. He'd popped his head through the bars of the gate and chewed the antlers straight from her head.

I couldn't help laughing as I went over to give her a hand. I'd known those antlers wouldn't last.

'Look, he just wants to wear them. He thinks he's a reindeer,' I said, giving Alan a stern look so he released the headband. Then I popped it over his head.

By now, all the other volunteers had stopped what they were doing and come over to see what the hilarity was all about. There was a roar of laughter as I stepped back to let Alan flaunt his new look.

The antlers bobbed about on his head, and he looked up at me as if to say, *I look really cute, don't I?* He was right too, he did look cute. On cue, he shook his head from side to side, jangling the little bells at the base of the antlers. We all fell about laughing again.

Eventually, after Alan had enjoyed his moment, I pulled the antlers back to the right side of the gate. He looked really disappointed. But at the back of my mind, an idea was forming. It was a Christmas idea too.

'Where did you get those?' I asked the girl with the antlers.

'Oh, these were from the supermarket,' she laughed. 'Why, do you fancy some for yourself now?'

Not me, no. But I knew a donkey who did.

'No reason,' I said. I wasn't going to let everyone in

on my little plan just yet. They wouldn't have taken me seriously anyway. I was too much of a Scrooge. Tracy catching the Christmas bug? Never.

'Lesley, you get the gates and make sure there's someone looking after the parking down there. Steve, you're on drinks. Everyone else, you know what you're doing. Apparently, it's time to have a party,' I said, manically pointing everyone to their posts.

The night had arrived and, whether I liked it or not, we were celebrating Christmas. I'd never admit it to Lesley and Steve, but the idea had actually grown on me. Opening those Christmas cards was just the start of it. By the time I popped those antlers on Alan, I was almost feeling festive. I couldn't believe what had happened to me. I'd caught 'tinselitis'. That's the only explanation for the secret plan I had up my sleeve.

It started with that vision of Alan dressed up as a reindeer. I thought it would be a great surprise for the children to turn up and find that my donkeys had been swapped for something more festive. So I'd signed into eBay to have a look for some more antlers. I popped them into my virtual shopping basket, and I was about to shell out for extortionate express delivery when something else down at the bottom of the page caught my eye.

It was a model, dressed up from head to toe in a daft elf outfit. It looked ridiculous. She was wearing red and white striped tights, a gaudy green and red tunic dress, and a silly elf hat. Instead of scoffing at the stupidity and clicking off the website, the Christmas bug whispered in my mind.

Wouldn't it be funny if I turned up at the party dressed as an elf? No one would believe it. That would show them I could have fun too. Should I do it?

In a festive trance, I added the outfit to my shopping basket and before I could talk myself out of it I was typing in my card details. The spirit of Christmas took over, and I clicked to complete the transaction. It was too late to have second thoughts. It was done.

I decided not to tell anyone what I was planning. Even Steve was kept in the dark. When the postman arrived I stashed the package away in the office so he wouldn't find it. It was still there now.

Down at the bottom of the drive, cars started pulling in and parking up. I turned around and gave the local brass band the nod to start playing. If I was going to host a Christmas party, I was going to give it a bit of a wow factor. The band were delighted to be invited, and had come ready with a full set list of carols and Christmas songs. Then, as the familiar sounds of

'Rudolph the Red-Nosed Reindeer' rang out across the yard, it was time for me to get ready.

'Say hello to people, I'll be back in a few minutes,' I said to Steve, dashing off before he could question why.

I grabbed the package from the office and upstairs in the bedroom I ripped it open. Out tumbled my outfit for the night, just as I'd ordered it.

'Right, let's do this,' I said, pushing my feet through the unattractive tights.

I pulled the tunic over my head then ran a brush through my hair before yanking the pointy hat down on top. I looked at myself in the mirror and burst out laughing. I looked absolutely ludicrous.

I could hear the crowds gathering outside, but there was just time for the final touch. I grabbed a tube of red lipstick from my pitiful make-up collection, and swirled two red circles for rosy cheeks. Time to face the music – literally.

As soon as I stepped back out into the yard, laughter started to ripple through the crowd as people caught sight of me. I saw Lesley do a double take, a confused look on her face before she twigged it was me.

'I'm speechless. Is that really you?' she said, coming straight over to see for herself.

'Erm, yes, I thought it would be funny,' I said.

'Well, it is. But you hate Christmas,' she said, still confused.

'Don't tell anyone but it's beginning to grow on me,' I replied, as I took in the atmosphere. Hundreds of people had turned up, and already everyone was laughing and chatting, having a great time.

Over in the stables Alan and a couple of his pals were jazzed up with the reindeer antlers. Just as I expected, the children loved it. Alan couldn't get enough of the attention. The barbecue had been fired up and the brass band was the icing on the cake.

I mingled with the crowds, wishing a very happy Christmas to all the sanctuary's local supporters. The number of compliments I received on my outfit was astonishing. You'd have thought I was wearing a designer frock, not some tat from eBay. People loved the effort I'd gone to.

After a while, I checked my watch. It was almost time for the second surprise of the night. We were welcoming a very special guest, straight from the North Pole. Well, kind of. Ross had agreed to dress up as Santa and I thought it would be fun for him to make a bit of an entrance.

I headed into the far stable, where Ross was getting ready.

'All set?' I asked. He certainly looked the part. He's a

big guy and he filled out the Santa suit to perfection. Once he'd popped the beard on you wouldn't have known it was him.

'I've been practising my "ho ho ho",' he joked.

'Great. I'll just check on your escorts,' I said.

Santa couldn't turn up on his own. He needed some reindeer. Unfortunately the party's special effects budget didn't stretch as far as a proper sleigh. But Alan and his friend Teddy would definitely help with the wow factor.

In the next stable Lesley had fastened Teddy and Alan into festive red head collars. They were ready to go too.

'Right, Alan, you just behave yourself. Remember this was all your idea,' I said, giving him his orders. If he hadn't been pratting around with that reindeer head-band, I would never have had the inspiration.

Alan looked up at me as if to say, *Trouble? Me?* There was no time for a rethink. This was Alan's moment, whether he was ready for it or not. So I took the ropes, handed them over to Ross, and gathered the crowds ready.

'Please welcome tonight's special guest. He's very busy this time of year, but he's made a special trip just for us. It's Father Christmas,' I shouted, as Ross made his way around the corner.

Teddy was on one side and Alan was on the other.

They looked an absolute picture. The trio started making their way over towards the makeshift Santa's grotto, as the littlest children screamed with excitement.

But after just a few steps, I could see there was going to be a problem. A great big donkey-sized problem. I saw Alan catch sight of a bloke munching on a juicy burger, while his kids stood in front waving at Santa. His attention wavered, and then he stopped dead in his tracks.

'Oh bugger. Please, Alan. Don't do this,' I muttered under my breath.

Ross looked over to me desperately. He was tugging on the rope trying to get Alan to follow behind. Meanwhile, Teddy was completely focussed on the job at hand. He was a reindeer, and nothing was going to distract him.

Then Alan decided that rather than being a good boy and doing his job too, he'd prefer a bite of that burger. Ross couldn't do anything to stop him, as he headed off in completely the wrong direction. The crowd laughed nervously, while the bloke with the burger was completely oblivious to the fact that he was at the heart of the technical hitch.

I looked around for backup, panic rising. As usual, my right-hand woman Lesley was there when I needed her.

'Here, give him this,' she said, rummaging around in her coat pocket and producing a very stale ginger biscuit.

'This way, Alan, it's time Santa got to the grotto,' I said, leaping forward and waving the biscuit in front of his nose.

His nostrils twitched, and his eyes followed the path of the horrible limp cookie. He might have fancied sharing a burger for tea, but I knew that with donkeys a ginger biscuit would win any day.

I stepped backwards towards the grotto, and Ross gave Alan a subtle nudge forward with his leg. Then a collective sigh of relief rang out as Alan started plodding forwards again.

'That was close,' Ross whispered to me as he passed.

'You're telling me,' I said. 'Let's give out some of these presents before anything else goes wrong.'

Ross settled himself on a chair in the little grotto, with Alan and Teddy still by his side. I passed Alan the ginger biscuit to munch down. I hoped it would be enough of an incentive for him to behave.

A queue of children snaked through the yard to see Santa. One by one, they whispered to Ross what was on their Christmas lists while the parents snapped a photo as a memento. I was gasping for a mulled wine to take the edge off the stress, but I didn't dare leave Alan just yet.

The first ten or fifteen children passed through the grotto with no problems. Alan minded his own business and Ross promised to make their Christmas wishes come true. The party was back on track.

But just as I was thinking it might be safe for me to retreat for some adult company, Christmas took a nose-dive again.

Ross had just leaned down to ask a little blonde girl what she was hoping to find under the tree when Alan decided that eating only one measly ginger biscuit had left him a bit peckish. No burgers in sight, he picked the next best thing to satisfy his appetite. That just happened to be Ross's fake white fluffy beard.

He swooped his head forward and grabbed the fluff between his front teeth. Ross immediately whipped his hands up to hold on to it. The mum, seeing the trouble unfold, dashed up and grabbed her little girl, shielding her eyes from the uncovering of Santa. It was chaos. Just as he had with the model's bikini in Sutton-on-Sea, Alan decided that it was the perfect time for a game of tug of war. Ross, with the loop of elastic still around his head, tugged back.

'No, Alan, no!' I shouted, grabbing hold of the beard too. Together Ross and I gave it a big yank and Ross nearly fell backwards off his chair as Alan released it from his jaws.

'Stable, now,' I hissed at Ross, seeing the state the beard was in. 'Cover your face so the children don't see.'

He hustled off to fix his disguise, leaving me to deal with Alan.

'I've had enough of you,' I said. 'I gave you a special job because I thought you deserved it, but you've blown it. You're out of the grotto, come on.'

I pulled him back out into the crowds, where he couldn't do any more damage to Ross's beard. Kids were still queuing to get in and the parents were looking at me expectantly. It was time to improvise.

'Santa's just having a quick break. Why don't we sing some carols to welcome him back?' I suggested, catching the eye of the brass band conductor.

He gave me the nod, and led the band in a soothing rendition of 'Silent Night'. The crowd started to sing along and, slowly, my heart rate returned to somewhere close to normal. Ross would put his beard on, I'd get Alan out of the way, and everything would be fine.

Then, just as the band launched into the second verse of the carol, an almighty bray drowned out the music. The children covered their ears in distress, and the adults winced at the racket. I didn't even need to look down beside me to see what was going on. It was Alan, again. This time, he fancied a singalong. But with a voice like that he'd leave us all deaf.

I turned my head to catch his eye with a steely glare, just in time to see him snaffle a mince pie straight out of an unsuspecting boy's hand. Alan sprayed crumbs everywhere, as tears welled in the kid's eyes.

'He stole my pie,' the child said, pointing at Alan accusingly. Then he burst into noisy, snotty tears.

Enough was enough. Alan had ruined my party. He'd wrecked Santa's grand entrance, before nearly disastrously revealing that Santa wasn't even real. He'd shattered everyone's ears by trying to join in the singalong, before leaving children in tears with his greedy appetite. I completely regretted involving Alan in the first place. I should have left him in the yard with the other donkeys.

I pulled him out of the crowd and, my blood boiling, handed him over to Steve.

'Keep him out of my sight. That bloody donkey is a nightmare.' I stormed off to finally get myself a much-needed mulled wine – or four. The party had been a disaster, and it was all Alan's fault.

An hour later, I'd finally simmered down enough to relax. Dare I say it, I was actually having a good time, as long as no one mentioned the D-word to me. Donkey. There's that saying that you should never work with children or animals. That evening had certainly proved it to be true.

'We're just about to leave but I wanted to thank you for having us before we do,' a woman said, approaching me from the crowd.

I didn't really recognise her, or the small boy in wellies trailing behind her. She must have been a guest from the village.

'Oh, you're welcome. It was nothing really. Did you have fun?' I asked.

'Definitely. My son loved the donkeys. It's made his Christmas. We'll be back for a proper visit when you're open again,' she said, smiling at her son who'd wandered off a few metres behind me.

I heard a childish giggle behind my back, and a snuffly growling noise too. I turned around to see Alan nudging at the boy with his head as he stroked him. Trust Alan to be loitering around still. The evening was drawing to a close, so I told myself that he couldn't cause much more trouble.

'Oh, he's made a friend,' the mum laughed. 'He loves animals more than people. It's a shame he didn't get to see Santa earlier, but he was feeling a bit shy.'

Then the giggling came again. Alan pushed the boy

forwards a couple of steps towards his mum. The boy tugged on her sleeve, and gestured for her to bend down so he could whisper something to her.

'I think I want to see Santa now,' I heard him say.

'Oh, well, I'll have to ask this lady if Santa's still here. He might have had to get back to the North Pole,' the mum said, giving me a knowing look.

'I'm sure Santa's still here somewhere,' I said, looking around for Ross. 'Let me see if I can catch him before he has to go.'

Then the little boy tugged on his mum's sleeve again.

'He says he'd feel happier seeing Santa if your donkey can come with him,' she laughed.

Alan looked up at me as if to say, *Well, can I?* He knew very well he'd been banned from the grotto for his bad behaviour but how could I say no?

'Go on then,' I said, resigned. 'I'll go and find Santa.'

Ten minutes later Ross had pulled the itchy beard back on, and was waiting ready in the grotto. The little boy sidled up to him, with Alan close behind. I could have sworn Alan gave him a nod, as if to say it was okay to go ahead.

He whispered his Christmas wish in Ross's ear, then Ross rummaged in the sack to find him a little present. I was poised ready to yank Alan back out of the grotto at the smallest hint of any of his funny business. But this time he was as good as gold.

The boy ran back to his mum, beaming from ear to ear.

'Thanks so much,' she said. 'I don't think he would have gone in if it hadn't been for your donkey.'

I realised she was right. Alan had given him the confidence to go out of his comfort zone. At least one little boy would remember my Christmas party for the right reasons.

I said goodbye to them and turned to see Alan looking at me smugly. He'd known exactly what he was doing. He wanted to make up for his bad behaviour earlier.

'What am I going to do with you?' I said, rubbing his head affectionately. I'd never met a donkey who could make me feel so enraged then so happy in such a short space of time. Alan was definitely a one-off.

'I think it's time to call it a night,' Steve said. 'We've eaten everything and drunk everything.'

'I agree. I'm knackered,' I said. 'The vicar's going to say a few words, then hopefully everyone will get the hint and bugger off.'

'Don't you dare pretend you've had enough of parties. I saw you, you were having fun,' Steve said teasingly.

'All right, I suppose I was. But now I need my bed,' I said. 'And I can't wait to get this blooming elf outfit off.'

So I went off to find the vicar from the local church. He hushed the crowd before giving a festive blessing, wishing us all a very happy Christmas.

Then, to my relief, people started to make their way towards the gates.

'Bye, thanks for coming. Great to see you,' I smiled, as everyone filed past to say thank you.

'Sorry about Alan,' I added, catching the eye of the parents of the kid whose mince pie he'd rudely pinched.

'Don't worry at all. He's over it now, and can't wait to tell his friends about the donkey he met,' the dad said with a grin.

'Alan, is that his name?' another visitor chimed in. 'He really made my night. I've never heard a donkey sing before.'

'Don't remind me,' I said, cringing at the memory of Alan belting out carols.

'Honestly, he was hilarious. Best Christmas party I've been to in years.'

I blushed at that compliment. People could be very forgiving. But as I carried on saying my goodbyes Alan kept coming up again and again.

Mums thought it was hilarious that he'd tried to eat Ross's beard, and the children were giggling at when my naughty 'donkey reindeer' tried to escape from Santa. Even the brass band players joked that maybe he could be their honorary member.

By the time I closed the gate behind the last partygoer, it had dawned on me that perhaps Alan hadn't ruined my party after all. He'd made it. While I'd been tearing my hair out at his antics, everyone else had completely fallen for his cheeky charm. They'd all loved him. In fact, if it hadn't been for Alan, the party would have been a bit dull. At least everyone was going home with funny memories, and stories to tell. He'd made everyone smile. I supposed that that was what Christmas was really about.

I locked the gate, and trudged back up the drive replaying the evening in my mind. The look on Ross's face when Alan tried to go after that burger made me smirk. And the grimaces when he'd joined in the singing were classic. I felt really lucky to have celebrated Christmas surrounded by my nearest and dearest, including my menagerie of animals. If it hadn't been for Alan, I probably wouldn't have had the party in the first place. But, thanks to him, it had been one to remember. I was starting to think that maybe Christmas wasn't so bad after all.

15

The Best Present Ever

A week later and we were all still talking about the party. Every time we remembered Alan's not-so-grand entrance we dissolved into fits of laughter.

'You were furious, though, Tracy. You should have seen your face,' Lesley said, as we reminisced during our 11 a.m. coffee break on Christmas Eve.

'No I wasn't. I was only mildly concerned,' I protested.

'Yeah, right. You looked like you wished you'd never laid eyes on Alan,' Lesley said with a grin.

'Well, okay. I suppose I wasn't that happy with him. But he nearly ruined the whole thing,' I said, breaking out into giggles again at the image of Ross stuck in the middle with my steady Teddy on one side of him and naughty Alan on the other. 'All is forgiven now, though. He gave everyone a laugh at least.'

'He sure did. But you know what this means? There's no way you'll get out of a repeat performance next year.

I think the Radcliffe Donkey Sanctuary Christmas party should be an annual occasion,' Lesley teased. 'You could get the elf costume out again.'

'I don't know about that. The stress nearly sent me over the edge. Let's get this Christmas out of the way first,' I said.

The party hadn't been enough to turn me into Mrs Christmas. I wasn't going to dash out to the shops to buy a tree the size of a small mountain, and fork out a fortune for armfuls of stupid gifts. I didn't have the time, and neither did I want to. However, for the first time since being a kid I felt vaguely festive and I had to admit I liked it.

The rest of Christmas Eve passed without event. By the time the sun went down the donkeys were safely in their stables, snoozing while they waited for Santa. I'd taken all the money that people had kindly donated for their Christmas pressies, and restocked the fun side of the tack room. They'd wake up to some heavy duty horse balls to play with. Their favourite.

My Christmas Eve was probably quite different to most people's. There were no guests to welcome, vegetables to prep, or turkey to defrost. That was the way I liked it. Christmas Day was usually the only day of the year that Steve and I spent by ourselves. No volunteers, no fuss, nothing. There wasn't anything I could do about the donkeys, though; I was stuck with them whether I liked it or not.

That night we enjoyed the luxury of an early night. It might not have felt like Christmas, but to me, snuggled up at home with my husband and a gaggle of donkeys outside, it was just perfect.

The next morning I was up bright and early. But not to see what Santa had brought me. I had my donkeys to look after.

I headed out into the yard and let them into the fields. As usual, they were far too excited about going out to play to even acknowledge me.

'Fine then, you'll change your tune in a minute,' I stropped, heading back to the tack room and grabbing a bucket on the way. I picked up a couple of cans of Guinness waiting there for me on the worktop, and cracked them open. They weren't for me, though. Even on Christmas Day I didn't get on the booze that early. The Guinness was for the donkeys. It wasn't my drink of choice but they loved it.

The Guinness had become a bit of a Christmas ritual. Every year I filled up a couple of buckets and took it down to the fields to give the donkeys a tipple. I'd be enjoying a glass or two of something alcoholic myself later, and it only seemed fair that the donkeys got to indulge as well.

I plodded back down to the fields, the Guinness slopping around in the buckets I had over each arm. Surprise surprise, Alan was there waiting at the fence for me.

'How did you know about this?' I asked. This was his first Christmas at the sanctuary, so there was no way he could have known I'd be heading back over. Unless the other donkeys had tipped him off, I supposed. Alan's sixth sense of when treats were arriving never failed to amaze me. He was still always first at the fence when we had visitors in, kicking on the gate to make sure he got all the fuss and the first bite of the carrots.

He gave me a little look, as if to say, *Am I going to get my treat then?*

'Go on then, get your nose in that,' I said, holding the bucket out for him to have a noisy slurp. He lifted his head back out, froth dripping from his nose and a look of pure pleasure on his face.

'You liked that, did you?' I said, laughing at him. 'Go on then, have another gulp, but don't tell the others. They'll accuse me of having favourites.

'No more, that's your lot,' I said, rubbing his nose affectionately.

To think that Alan had only come into my life thanks to fate. If he hadn't been abandoned, or that woman had phoned a different donkey sanctuary or, heaven forbid, we hadn't been able to save his life, it would have been a different story. I'd never have met him. And as I thought about all his adventures over the past year since he'd arrived, I realised my life would be a much bleaker one without him. Sure, I would have fewer grey hairs and I'd probably sleep better at night. But when faced with the alternative of a life without Alan, I wouldn't have it any other way.

It seemed so long ago that he'd arrived as a scrawny, sad little donkey. Yet, I vividly remembered how frightened I'd been that he wouldn't survive. He'd been so weak and damaged. And all those hours I spent trying to tempt him out of the stable to make friends seemed like a distant memory. He hadn't been the same cheeky Alan I'd come to know and love. It had been a privilege to see him become the donkey he now was.

He'd had quite the year. He'd starred in a fashion shoot, made friends with thousands of visitors, saved Dona Pepa not just once but twice, come to the rescue when the vandals had struck, and then rounded it off with his farcical performance at the Christmas party. Most of my donkeys don't have that many adventures in their lifetime. Alan is different, though. I have a funny feeling that drama will follow him around wherever he goes. Fortunately for me, he isn't going anywhere. He has a long and happy life ahead of him at the sanctuary, and I'll get to enjoy all those adventures with him.

As I reminisced I felt really emotional. I was so lucky to have the life that I did. Running the sanctuary wasn't always fun, and it certainly wasn't always easy, but having Alan around to perk up my day made it all worthwhile . . .

My daydream was suddenly shattered by the arrival of the rest of the Hooligans. There was no way they'd let Alan slurp down all of my Guinness by himself. I held the bucket over the fence so they could each have a sip, before heading off around the sanctuary to wish a happy Christmas to the other donkeys.

Christmas Day could have come to an end right there and then for all I cared. Spending quality time with my donkeys would be the highlight for me.

In truth, it was a good job that it was only 9 a.m. There was work to be done, just as there was on the other 364 days of the year. The only difference was that Steve and I had to get through the tick list ourselves. Any one of our volunteers would have driven straight over if we'd needed them, Christmas Day or no Christmas Day. But it seemed only fair that they got at least one day of peace a year. Steve and I would be mucking out the stables by ourselves.

But first, we had a Christmas ritual of our own to indulge. Steve was already prepared for it.

'Ready to go?' he asked, coming towards me with two flasks of hot coffee.

'Yep. I could do with that coffee,' I said, taking both off him as we climbed into the car.

Steve started the engine and we ambled three miles down the countryside roads to the coast. We parked up at Huttoft car terrace, a car park right on the beach. All that separated us from the sand was a short concrete barrier, to stop cars accidentally rolling down into the sea. There was a wide stretch of unblemished yellow sand, and beyond that the waves crashed rhythmically. Every Christmas Day we went down there for half an hour of peace. It was bliss.

Steve cranked his seat backwards and stretched his legs out.

'We should do this more often,' he sighed.

I laughed. We said that every year, without fail. Yet we never seemed to find the time.

'Well, when we win the lottery and hire an army of helpers we can relax down here every day. But until then, you're stuck at the sanctuary with me and the donkeys, I'm afraid,' I said, gulping down my coffee.

'Hmm, I'll keep my fingers crossed then.'

What we'd do if we won the lottery was a long-running

joke. I'd already made my mind up, just in case it ever happened. There was no way I was giving up the donkey sanctuary to become a lady of leisure. Instead, it would be bigger and better than ever. We'd buy up the neighbouring fields, and finally find the money to build a big hay barn. Every donkey in need would be welcome, no matter where they were in the world. I'd pay to have them shipped from Timbuktu if I had to. All of our long-suffering volunteers would be given a generous wage, with a huge bonus to make up for all the years they'd put up with my donkeys with no reward other than lunch. Finally, I was pretty certain I still wouldn't be taking another day off. Travelling the world wasn't for me. I was quite happy with my peaceful little corner of Lincolnshire.

Steve's belly interrupted my wishful thinking with a loud grumble.

'Hungry?' I asked.

'Always. Surely it's time for that fry-up?' he replied.

That was the second part of our Christmas ritual, a big greasy fry-up with the full works. And now Steve had mentioned it, I was ready to tuck in too.

It was a good job we'd had that fry-up. We needed it. Mucking out all the stables before darkness fell was a big job. I'd topped up the hay and refilled the water with only minutes to spare. We herded the donkeys back in for bed and, to my relief, I saw that they hadn't completely destroyed the new horse balls yet.

With the donkeys peacefully tucked up for the evening, Steve and I could celebrate. I wasn't going to be whipping up a full turkey dinner with all the trimmings after the knackering day we'd had, but we usually had something a little bit special. I stuck a Tesco chicken in the oven along with some roasties, and prepped some carrots and asparagus to go alongside.

Then we put our feet up and popped open the bottle of bubbly we'd had chilling in the fridge since the morning. Finally we relaxed, and we'd certainly earned it.

After stuffing ourselves with roast dinner, we opened gifts from family and friends. Of course, there were always a few who'd ignored my requests and wrapped up a little something for me too. Then we flicked through the channels on the telly before settling on a Christmas special of some nonsense series we didn't usually watch. We opened a second bottle of booze and enjoyed a bit of time to ourselves.

By 10.30 p.m. my eyelids were drooping and we admitted defeat and headed to bed. It was an entirely typical Christmas Day for us, and I wouldn't have changed a thing.

I opened my eyes and sat up, groaning at the pain that pounded through my temples. Suddenly that extra glass of wine didn't seem like such a good idea anymore. I didn't often have more than one and I was reminded why. I couldn't handle it.

I looked at my phone and swore under my breath. Six a.m. The donkeys would be desperate for their breakfast. They wouldn't care that it was Boxing Day, or that I needed a lie-in. So I stumbled my way downstairs, haphazardly lobbed some hay into the fields and let the residents out to amuse themselves for a while. The stables needed mucking out, but that could wait. I needed more sleep before I was fit for anything.

As I climbed back into bed, the effort made the room spin. Steve was still snoring away, completely oblivious to the fact that I'd even been away. I shut my eyes tightly, and prayed that when I woke up again my hangover would be gone.

Suddenly, the silence was shattered by the phone ringing downstairs.

Bleary-eyed, I groped my way out of bed and picked up the receiver.

'Hello,' I grunted. I had no idea what time it was, but it felt like I'd only drifted off again for a minute or two.

'Sorry, I just thought you might want to know that you've had an escape,' the man on the other end said, without introducing himself.

'I've what? Huh?' I said. Whatever time it was, it was too early for cryptic conversation.

'Your donkeys,' he said. 'I live down in the village, and I've just opened my curtains to find one nibbling on my hedge.'

'Oh no,' I moaned. 'Sorry.'

'I'm assuming it's your donkey anyway. He seems to have brought some friends along too, and I don't know anyone else around here who keeps a herd of donkeys,' he said.

'I'm coming now,' I managed to say, before hanging up the phone and rubbing my sore head.

Even if there were any other donkeys living in the area, I was sure mine were the only ones naughty enough to escape. Trust them to pick today of all days. Chasing donkeys around the village certainly wasn't my idea of a hangover cure. A strong coffee, a bacon butty, and a few painkillers was more what I had in mind.

But it didn't look like I had any choice. I had to go and get the escapees back before they did any more damage.

'Steve, help!' I shouted up the stairs. 'We need to go.'

He emerged at the top of the staircase, looking as rough as I felt.

'What? You can't be serious?' he said grumpily.

'They've made a run for it again,' I said, keeping my

fingers crossed that only a couple had seized their chance of freedom.

Steve just sighed, and retreated back to the bedroom to find some clothes.

I looked down at my pink pyjama bottoms and decided that getting changed was more trouble than it was worth. If I set foot anywhere near my bed, there was a very real danger I'd get back under the covers and never get out again. Pink PJs seemed as good as anything for donkey hunting.

So I pulled on a pair of wellies, before realising to my dismay that one was black and one was green. Oh well. The people of Huttoft could have a good laugh at me.

I thrust a couple of packets of ginger biscuits into my pocket and waited for Steve out in the yard. Then together, mumbling and grumbling, we checked the fields to work out who had gone missing.

My Geriatrics were all present and correct – no surprise there. I doubted they would make a run for it even if I'd left the gate wide open for them. They knew which side their bread was buttered. When you get to old age what more would you want than a cosy bed for the night and a ready supply of food?

The Mismatches were all pratting around as usual too. But with horror I realised the Hooligans' field was completely empty. Alan and twelve of his naughty donkey pals were gone.

It wasn't the first time it had happened, and I was sure it wouldn't be the last. Sometimes I wondered whether those donkeys kept a secret supply of power tools stashed in the bushes, as they seemed to have a knack of getting the gates off the hinges. That day the timing couldn't have been worse.

'I bet they've done it on purpose just to wind me up,' I groaned to Steve. 'I'll grab the head collars.'

Any hope of a little lie-in to soothe my aching head was long gone. When the Hooligans embarked on an adventure they would not be easily tempted back. The trouble with keeping the naughtiest donkeys together was that they egged each other on. I could bet Alan was the ringleader, though. Deciding to get up to mischief on the one day I really needed him not to was exactly his type of game.

A few minutes later Steve and I shuffled down the road into the village. Thankfully, with it being Boxing Day, no one else seemed to be up and about yet.

'Where shall we start?' Steve asked, looking around for any sign that our donkeys were about.

'The bloke said he lived by the pub, so let's work from there,' I said.

We plodded down towards the Axe and Cleaver just

in time to see a donkey's arse disappear around the corner, heading up the long untarmacked driveway opposite.

'I reckon that was Billy,' I panted, jogging across the road brandishing a head collar.

Steve followed close behind. We caught Billy with his head in the hedge, having a good look to see what grub he could find.

'No you don't, you're coming with me,' I said, fastening the head collar before he even had time to realise the game was over.

One down, eleven to go.

'Up here, Tracy,' Steve called to me from further up the driveway.

Of course it was Dolly Daydream. If Billy was around, she'd never be far. They were like a match made in heaven. So, tugging Billy behind me, I went up to pass Steve a second head collar. He wasted no time in capturing her too.

Dolly Daydream was the one donkey I knew would be no trouble to capture. She'd never known anything but kindness as she was actually born at the sanctuary. She had complete trust in humans. Her mother, Josephine, was dumped at the sanctuary one afternoon back in 1995. She was old and incredibly thin. In fact, when the vet saw her he said, 'If I had a vase as old as that donkey, I'd be rich.' We started an intensive rota to refeed her, gradually building her strength. Thankfully it worked.

Then one day I was brushing the mud from her legs when I noticed that she had started developing udders. Alarm bells went off in my head. Surely she couldn't be pregnant? But when I worked out the dates it was entirely possible she'd been in the early weeks of pregnancy when she arrived. A donkey pregnancy could last as long as fourteen months, and swollen udders were a sure sign that birth was imminent. It wasn't something I'd had an opportunity to see before as I'd never had a pregnant donkey. I'd read about it, though.

We called the vet back out, who was delighted to see how healthy Josephine was now. But he confirmed that yes, somehow, she was pregnant. In June 1996 little Dolly Daydream was born, and Josephine was a fantastic mother. She died in 2008, but our Dolly Daydream was a real credit to her. She was a lovely donkey.

'You take these two back, and I'll keep hunting,' I said to Steve, passing him Billy's rope.

'Okey-dokey,' Steve said.

'You better come back, though. No stopping for a sneaky coffee or a lie down,' I threatened.

Then I decided to have a look around at the back of the pub. I crept across the car park at the front, and headed out of the view of the road. There I found Buster, exploring a dangerous-looking pile of rubble. He was always last to bed at night, but he would never pass up an opportunity for a little outing.

'No, Buster, you'll hurt yourself,' I warned, as he tentatively placed his foot on top of the pile of old bricks.

He looked back at me as if he was trying my patience, like a naughty child who wanted to do the one thing that their mum said they couldn't. But I wasn't going to give him the chance to find out what happened if he disobeyed me. I fastened the head collar, and pulled him out of harm's way.

'Now, where are your friends?' Even if Buster could talk, I knew there was no way he'd give them up. He was enjoying the fun and games far too much.

I started to make my way to the front of the pub, to see if Steve was on his way back. I looked up just in time to see a donkey pop his head around the corner, see that I was on the warpath, and retreat immediately.

I'd know that cheeky little face anywhere. It was Alan, but I couldn't chase him without letting go of Buster. I yanked on the rope and pulled Buster after me. Alan was still loitering at the front of the pub. It was like he was daring me to try to capture him. He knew he had the upper hand. But what he hadn't banked on was how well I knew him. I couldn't chase him, he was right about that. However, I did have the one thing he wanted. Treats.

I rustled in my pocket with my spare hand, producing a handful of ginger biscuits.

'Look what I've got for you, yummy biscuits,' I said, holding them out in front of me so he could see.

His nostrils twitched, picking up the scent. He was tempted. So was Buster, who shoved his head towards my pocket, trying to nibble the rest of the packet. I passed him a biscuit to keep him quiet for a moment. My negotiation with Alan was reaching the crucial stage. Would he stay for a treat, or would he leg it?

'Do you want one?' I asked, lobbing a biscuit out on the ground a couple of metres away from me.

Of course he stayed for a biscuit. With only a second's thought, he stepped forward and gulped it down. I breathed a sigh of relief as I spotted Steve at the far end of the road. I only had to keep Alan occupied for a few more moments.

'Look, I've got lots more,' I said, waving my handful of crumbs again.

I threw another out to him, a bit closer to where I was stood this time. Again, he fell for it, and gobbled it down. Steve was closer, and I gave him a desperate look to hurry up. So while I distracted Alan with a third biscuit Steve came up from behind with the head collars he'd taken from Dolly Daydream and Billy. Before Alan knew what was going on, we'd caught him.

At first he looked horrified that I'd tricked him. Then a look of resignation came over him. It was the end of his adventure. He glanced behind him, and I saw the faces of four more of my donkeys peering out from an open front garden down the road.

That confirmed everything I needed to know. Alan had been the boss of the whole escapade, and the rest of the donkeys were looking for him to tell them what their next move should be. Well, I had their ringleader now, so it was game over.

'Have you not caused enough trouble this Christmas?' I asked Alan. 'You had to ruin my Boxing Day too?'

He didn't even pretend to be sorry. I could tell he thought the whole thing was hilarious. I didn't agree. My headache was even worse than ever, and thanks to Alan and his friends I was pratting around in the village dressed in pyjamas and odd wellies.

Once I'd led Alan back to the safety of the sanctuary, it didn't take us long to round up the other escapees. We began leading the last few back just in time for the rest of the village to start waking up.

'You're up early,' one woman remarked, as she shifted a bin bag full of ripped-up wrapping paper out of her front door.

'Not by choice,' I said.

Then she looked down at my legs and caught sight of my pyjamas.

'I see what you mean,' she said, trying to hide her amusement.

Soon they were all back in the field with the gate firmly closed. I headed straight for the kitchen and stood there in a dilemma. Coffee first or bacon? Steve had the same thought.

'I'll put the kettle on, you get the butties on the go. We've earned them,' he said, grabbing some mugs.

As we tucked into our greasy hot baps my headache started to subside. And, to my surprise, I began to see the funny side.

'What a morning,' I chuckled

'You looked a right sight in those stupid pyjamas,' Steve said. 'It's a good job no one was up, or we'd never be able to show our faces down at the pub again.'

'Don't blame me, it was all blooming Alan's fault. I'm sure this whole thing was his idea,' I said. 'He picks on me.'

'Yeah, yeah.' Steve rolled his eyes at my conspiracy theory.

It was true, though. He'd been determined to cause chaos all Christmas. Ruining the Christmas party hadn't been enough for him. He wasn't going to let me relax on Boxing Day either. I was just surprised that Christmas Day had been so quiet.

But when I thought about the past few weeks, I realised that I hadn't smiled so much in months. Alan's antics had made my Christmas one to remember, once I'd got over the stress of it all. It was the best Christmas gift I could have had. Nearly a year before, I'd given him the gift of life, scooping him up from that dingy little car park and bringing him home for a life of countryside bliss. He'd given me the perfect present in return – the gift of love and laughter.

Epilogue

It would have been great if life had settled down for a while, after the Christmas chaos was behind us. I certainly deserved a bit of time to put my feet up. Deep down I knew there was no chance of that, though. Not with Alan around.

He revelled in his festive antics for a while. It certainly cemented his position as the sanctuary's number one troublemaker. I could have sworn the little bugger had a bit of a spring in his step in the weeks that followed, as if he was proud of having given me the runaround. And it wasn't long before he was back to making mischief again.

But then something happened that rocked our world to the very core. Dona Pepa, Alan's closest friend, passed away. This time, there was nothing he could do to save her. I could tell by the vacant look in her eyes that we were losing her. Norrie tried her best to revive her, but her time had come. I made her as comfortable as I could and lay down next to her in the stable. Then she let out a sigh and with that she was gone. I cried and cried, and I could tell that Alan was mourning too. He'd lost his partner in crime, and for a while his appetite for trouble vanished.

We were all feeling low when a pick-me-up came in an unlikely form. I'd rescued two zedonks, which are rare crosses between a zebra and donkey. Tigger and Humbug were bred in Holland to wild zebra mothers, and they shared a donkey dad. They'd been imported to a farm park in Dorset, but when that closed down the owner was at a loss for what to do with them. The genetic mix had left them almost untameable, so he was struggling to find anyone who'd take them in.

As usual, I couldn't refuse an animal in need, so the pair were transported up to Lincolnshire to join the rest of my motley crew. At first they wouldn't let me near them. They didn't trust humans, and would happily have trampled me. They were turned out into their own separate field every day to amuse themselves, then returned to the stable yard at night. At least they were safe, warm and being fed. But then one morning I was shocked to see that the stable yard was empty. The gates were closed; however, somehow the zedonks had completely disappeared.

My panic only subsided when I found them both in the bottom field, grazing with a group of donkeys. We managed to round Tigger and Humbug up, but it wasn't long before they were showing off their new trick again. They'd learned to jump the gate. It was obvious that they'd decided they wanted to make friends with my donkeys. I'd been worried their behaviour would be too rough, but I was soon proved wrong.

For some reason, Tigger took a liking to my little Alan. They were a perfect pairing. Alan was happy to indulge Tigger's rough and tumble games, and the friendship seemed to calm Tigger's temper too. I felt hugely relieved. I didn't care whether Tigger liked me or not, as long as I was offering him a better quality of life. Seeing him rolling around on the ground with Alan made me certain he was happy.

Nowadays, Tigger and Alan are completely inseparable. Alan has retired from the Hooligans, and lives happily with Tigger and the rest of the Mismatches. That's not to say he's grown up at all, though. He still causes more trouble than I'd ever have guessed a little donkey could. As always he gives the customers the sad eyes to lure them over with their buckets of carrots, but he's not fooling me. I know exactly what he's up to, and the glint in his eye tells me that he knows I'm on to him.

Alan certainly hasn't learnt any lessons from his first year of escapades at the sanctuary. Just a few months ago I went out one morning to find that it had absolutely chucked it down overnight. The fields were sodden and flooded in places, and most of the donkeys were sticking to the safety of drier ground. But not my Alan. He'd managed to paddle all the way up to his belly, finding the deepest puddle in the field. It was as if Dona Pepa's ordeal in the dyke had taught him nothing. I immediately leaped in and dragged him out, and he plodded reluctantly behind me. He hadn't been in any difficulty; he just wanted to give me a scare. Nothing's changed there.

He's also proved himself to be just as nosy as ever. He hates the thought that there could be any drama going on at the sanctuary without him being involved. Even when Miss Ellie, our huge American Jackstock mare, went into labour he was trying to poke his head into the stable to get a look at the action. Most blokes would have run a mile, but not my Alan.

Miss Ellie had been pregnant when she came to live at the sanctuary, and waiting for the birth was the most stressful time I've ever had. I even got Steve to set up a CCTV link to her stable so I could keep an eye on her from the house in the evening. I called it Ellievision, and it became addictive viewing. Eventually she gave birth to a little male foal we named Derrick, and Steve got stuck in to help with the delivery. I could tell Alan was disappointed that it wasn't his moment of glory. He was certainly making his presence felt outside with his noisy bray.

Elsewhere at the sanctuary, our fields are fuller than ever. It's bittersweet for me. I love seeing the donkeys prancing around, enjoying life. It's what they should be doing. They shouldn't be languishing alone in a paddock, or locked in a shed, or being plumped up for the slaughterhouse. But taking in a new resident usually means that they've been mistreated or let down in some way by someone else. There's no pleasure in that.

I feel so lucky to have the life that I do. It's a privilege to give the donkeys the opportunity to enjoy however many years they have left. People always ask me how I do it. How I cope with the long hours, the stress, and the fact I've never had another day off since my excursion to Twycross Zoo. My answer is always that I don't need a day off and I don't want a day off. It's easy to get out of bed when you're waking up to the possibility of making a difference. I need them just as much as they need me really.

That's why this Christmas, as at every Christmas, I'll be giving thanks for the things that are important to me. My family, my friends, and of course my donkeys. Alan's been invited to take part in a local nativity, and

I'm still in two minds about whether he's up to the job. His naughty antics might prove too much for the kids to handle. Whatever happens, though, there's no doubt how I'll be celebrating on Christmas Day. I'll be up bright and early in the fields giving Alan and his friends their festive tipple, although I'll be hoping that won't inspire another escape plot this year. Christmas is a time to spend with your loved ones, and there's nowhere I'd rather be.

Acknowledgements

Having the opportunity to put Alan's adventures down on paper has been an absolute pleasure. On a day-to-day basis I'm so busy mucking out stables, tricking donkeys into taking their medicine, and planning my next rescues that it's not often I get time to reflect. At the end of the day I flop into bed, ready to get up at 5.30 a.m. to do it all again. But reliving Alan's antics has given me no end of laughter. The memories of that bikini photoshoot and his Christmas party shenanigans really are priceless, and I hope they make readers smile too.

None of this would have been possible without the help of Danielle Hoffman, who helped me to put my story into words. I have to thank Ingrid Connell and the rest of the team at Pan Macmillan, as well as my literary agent Clare Hulton. I would also like to express my gratitude to Jack Falber for his hard work behind the scenes to make this possible, as well as Helen O'Brien for her valuable input and for proofreading the drafts of the manuscript.

Special thanks must also go to my long-suffering husband, Steve. He only had a budgie before he met me, so he certainly never expected to be sharing his home with so many noisy, smelly donkeys. But he has supported and helped me in every single step I've taken to build the Radcliffe Donkey Sanctuary into what it is today. Without him, hundreds of donkeys wouldn't have had their second chance at life.

I am also grateful from the bottom of my heart to all the volunteers who have spared their time and energy to help at the sanctuary. I am especially thankful to those who put their faith in what I was trying to achieve right at the beginning, in particular Becky Wade, Laura Stokes, Alex Brown, Sue and Brian Broughton, and not forgetting Kath Thompson, who stayed with us for a week to help the animals settle in when we moved to Huttoft. She still travels from Radcliffe-on-Trent to help me now.

Whether it's making cakes to sell in the cafe, helping me to capture the donkeys for a bath, or painting my fences, the volunteers are all worth their weight in gold. I must also thank my mum, Barbara, who still comes to help me out now, and my stepdad, Ken, who sadly died in 2004. He would have been so proud of everything we've achieved, and was always ready to dip into his pocket to pay for some donkey feed when times were desperate.

Without the expertise and patience of our vet, Norrie, our farrier, Russell, and our equine dentist, Tom, the donkeys wouldn't be living the happy, safe and pain-free lives that they do now. I couldn't count how many times I've been on the phone to them in an emergency, and they've always been ready to help.

Thanks also to all our customers. Without your kind donations there would be no Radcliffe Donkey Sanctuary.

I'm not the only one who owes a huge debt of gratitude to Muffin, the sanctuary's founding resident. When I rescued him it inspired me to change my life, taking it in a direction I never could have predicted. It is directly down to his influence that hundreds of donkeys have had a haven in which to live out the rest of their lives without cruelty, mistreatment or loneliness. I know that all of my residents would thank him for that.

And finally, thank you to Alan. There may be days when I wish he'd just pipe down and behave himself, but without his antics the sanctuary would be a much duller place to be. As well as a heap of stress, he's brought love and laughter into my life by the bucketload. I wouldn't have him any other way.

Support Alan

To support Alan and his friends, why not pay them a visit at the Radcliffe Donkey Sanctuary?

Radcliffe Donkey Sanctuary
Church Lane
Huttoft
Alford
Lincolnshire
LN13 9RB
Tel: 07940 146330 (daytime) or 01507 490864 (evening)

Opening days and times vary throughout the year, so please check on the website before making the trip.

Admission and parking are free, but donations are welcomed. Buying a bucket of carrots to feed the donkeys, or treating yourself to a cup of tea and a slice of cake in the cafe all helps towards the cost of looking after the donkeys and ensuring others in need can be rescued too.

For more information about the donkeys and the sanctuary, or to make a financial donation, visit www. radcliffedonkeys.com.

Adopt Your Favourite Donkey

Your favourite donkey needs you! Adopting a donkey for just £20 a year will help to keep him or her warm, healthy and well fed. You'll receive a special personalised certificate thanking you for your support. An adoption pack is the perfect gift too. For information about how to sign up for an adoption, please visit www.radcliffedonkeys.com or enquire when you visit the sanctuary.